Dividend Investing

The Ultimate Guide to Create Passive Income Using Stocks. Make Money Online, Gain Financial Freedom and Retire Early Earning Double-Digit Returns.

By Andrew Bennett

Respective authors own all copyrights not held by the publisher.

The information herein is offered for informational purposes solely, and is universal as so. The presentation of the information is without contract or any type of guarantee assurance.

The trademarks that are used are without any consent, and the publication of the trademark is without permission or backing by the trademark owner. All trademarks and brands within this book are for clarifying purposes only and are the owned by the owners themselves, not affiliated with this document.

Table of contents:

Introduction

You probably think first about stocks, shares, or mutual funds when you hear the term 'investing.' These are definitely among the most prevalent types that investments take, but investing is more than that.

Investing is about making more money from the capital. It is the most comfort description. There are many ways to invest, including:

- Bonds

- Stocks

- Precious metals

- Mutual Funds

- Real Estate

- Exchange-traded funds

- Trading currencies

You'll read about all these stuffs and more in this book. Behind those words you often hear on TV or view online, we'll open the mysteries: short trading, penny stocks, or economic indicators. You can hear from numerous markets, including the London Stock Exchange and the NASDAQ, as well as agencies, like the Reserve Bank and the Securities and Exchange Commission, and how investment decisions are influenced.

You'll hear how you can measure your risk tolerance. And from the best investors out there, you can hear the fundamentals.

Investing is a way to help you meet your ambitions, whether they pay for your education as well as for your kids, explore and have fresh and enjoyable experiences, or to finance a healthy retirement. You will broaden your investments and make your financial aspirations come true by spending wisely and well. There is an amazing universe out there packed with ways to earn profits, and it's ready for you to take advantage of it.

Chapter 1: Dividends and stocks

Dividends are income distributions that are not dependent on the stock price; they are rendered purely because the corporation has reaped good income and wishes to compensate shareholders. The board of directors may determine when and how much to offer a payout to shareholders, based on the company's earnings. For investors searching for income, dividends are typically the most significant, and stocks that give dividends are therefore classified as income stocks. Most businesses offer dividends on a quarterly pattern, and in some conditions, unusual one-time dividends can also be charged.

The phrase outstanding shares applies to the number of shares sold to the wider population, including its workers, by a corporation. Starting your investment career by gazing at firms with at least 5 million outstanding shares is a smart idea. This suggests that the stock is widely exchanged, which ensures that, there would be a ready buyer for them when you wish to sell your securities. More outstanding stock will imply smaller dividends per every shareholder at the same time (after all, there's just too much equity to go around), so bear that in mind while you're searching for stable profits.

Total Return

In terms of market shifts, most equity owners prefer to care about their profits and losses, not dividends, while those who buy bonds pay attention to interest rates and seldom concentrate on price changes. Both methods are incomplete. Although dividend returns could be more relevant if you are searching for revenue, and price increases are at the heart of growth stocks, the net return on every equity purchase is significant. Knowing the portfolio's overall return helps you equate your stock investments with other forms of stocks, such as corporate or local shares, treasuries, mutual funds, and investment trusts for groups.

Add the market price adjustment (or deduct it if the price has decreased) and dividends over the last twelve months to measure overall returns, and then divide by the price at the beginning of the twelve-month cycle. For, e.g., assume you purchase a share at $45 per share for the next twelve-month span and earn $1.50 in dividends. The stock would sell for $48 per share at the end of the time.

It will appear like this in your calculations: Dividend: $1.50

The shift of price: up to $3.00 per share

1,50 dollars + 3,00 dollars per share = 4,50 dollars

$4.50 broken by $45.00 = .10

A 10 percent raise is the net return.

Alternatively, assume that the price had fallen to $44 per share at the end of the time. Your proportions will then look like this:

Dividend: 1.50 dollar

A shift in price Down $1.00 per share

$1.50-$1.00 for each share = $0.50

$0.50 break by $45.00 = .0111

Just a 1.1 percent raise is the net return.

Analyze Dividends

You must legally purchase the stock in order to be entitled to dividends on the record date, which would be the day on which the board of directors announces a dividend. For the last five years, equate the present dividend with the dividends received. Shrinking dividends may imply expansion plans; dividends could be small or nonexistent when the primary objective of a business is development.

KINDS OF STOCKS What You Can Buy

The most prestigious, well-established corporations that are publicly listed, many of which have virtually become household brands, are called blue chips. General Electric (which trades on the NYSE under the symbol GE), McDonald's (NYSE: MCD), and Walmart are included in this mainly high cap combination (NYSE: WMT). For more than twenty-five years, many blue-chip corporations have operated and are now leading the pack in their respective sectors. They are decent investing opportunities for people leaning to the conservative side of their stock selections, as most of these companies have a strong track record.

Growth Stocks

Growth stocks involve businesses that have high growth prospects, which you would possibly infer by the term. Most firms have revenue, profits, and market share in this segment that are rising higher than the overall economy. In general, such stocks reflect firms that are high in R&D; for example, emerging technology leaders are also growth-stock companies. In these businesses, profits are typically placed straight back into the business rather than being paid out as dividends to shareholders.

Growth over Time

You would have paid $533 if you had bought 100 shares in Walmart in January of 1990. Your contribution will have been worth $1,144, more than 100 percent return, by January 1995. And by January 2014, $8,140 will have been worth your investment, more than ten times your initial buying price.

Growth stocks can be more expensive than their blue-chip equivalent, but you can still enjoy better incentives in certain situations. Usually speaking, in bull markets, growth stocks perform better (that is, when stock prices are generally rising), and in downturn markets, value stocks perform best (when stock prices are usually falling), although this is not assured. A note of caution: look out for securities that tend to be increasing quicker than might make sense. Momentum traders can also support sprint to sky-scraping heights of growth-stock rates, then sell them off, allowing the stock to plummet.

Income Stocks

Income stocks are exactly as the name suggests: they provide investors with stable income sources. These securities come with daily distributions of dividends, often high enough that individuals will potentially survive off their dividend checks. While several income stocks fall into the blue-chip group, consistent dividend dividends can still be provided by some kinds of stocks (like value stocks). These securities provide a fine addition to the holdings of fixed income since they often have the potential for appreciation in share prices.

Preferred Stocks

Preferred stocks have almost as much in common with bonds as they do with common stocks. This form of stock effectively comes with a maturity deadline and a set payout that gets charged irrespective of the firm's profits. If the corporation has financial difficulties, holders of preferred stock have priority when it comes to dividend payments. In times of prosperity, some preferred shares (called participating preferred) may get a second dividend payout that is based on earnings. As preferred stock owner, you normally don't have the rights that come with common stock ownership (like voting). However, preferred stock can be a good portfolio addition for income-oriented investors.

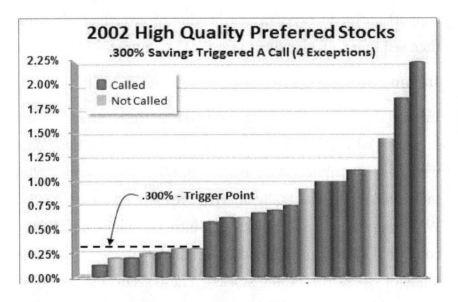

Small-, Mid-, and Large-Cap Stocks

A publicly traded corporation with 30 million outstanding shares currently trading for $20 each would have a market capitalization of $600 million. Although there are a few different groupings used to categorize stocks by their capitalization, here's a general rule of thumb you can follow:

- **Large-cap:** $10 billion and over

- **Mid-cap:** Between $2 billion and $10 billion

- **Small-cap:** Between $300 million and $2 billion

- **Micro-cap:** Under $300 million

Many small, developing firms that have overcome their initial growing pains and are now experiencing good earnings increases, along with increasing revenue and income, are part of the small-cap market segment. Today's small-cap stock maybe tomorrow's leader—it can also be tomorrow's loser. Overall, such stocks tend to be very volatile and risky. A safe way of adding these to your portfolio can be through a professionally managed small-cap fund. That way, you'll have exposure to potentially explosive profits without the added risk of investing in a particular company.

Mid-cap stocks, as the name suggests, are bigger than small-caps but smaller than large caps. Large-cap stocks are the biggest players in the stock market.

A large-cap corporation typically has a more solidly established presence and more reliable sales and profits than smaller corporations. Most of the time, larger companies make less risky investments than smaller companies; the tradeoff, though, can be slower growth rates. Most investors hold large-cap stocks for the long term, and for a good reason: more than fifty years of historical market returns show that these corporate giants yield only slightly lower returns than short-term investments, with much less volatility.

STOCKS

More Stock Types

Companies with earnings that are strongly tied to the business cycle are considered to be cyclical. When the economy picks up momentum, these stocks follow this positive trend. When the economy slows down, these stocks slow down, too. Cyclical stocks would include companies like United Airlines (NASDAQ: UAL).

On the other hand, defensive stocks, are relatively stable under most economic conditions, no matter how the market is faring. Stocks that fall into this category include food companies, drug manufacturers, and utility companies. For the most part, these companies produce things people can't live without, no matter what the economic climate is at any given time. The list of defensive stocks includes General Mills (NYSE: GIS) and Johnson & Johnson (NYSE: JNJ).

Reading Stocks

Any stock earns from the market on which it is traded a designation (this is easier than giving the full name of the company on a board or screen where space is limited). It is common when referring to a stock to offer the initials of the market in which it is exchanged, accompanied by a colon and the stock's sign.

As opposed to their corporate profits, dividends, revenue, or other fundamental considerations, value stocks look inexpensive. Essentially, you get better of what you're asking for: decent value. Value stocks appear to be overlooked while markets are high on growth stocks, rendering them much greater bargains for smart investors. Quality investors assume that in contrast to many growth stocks, these stocks allow better investments considering their fair price. Of course, a good value relies heavily on existing market values, so next month, a good value may not be a good value today. A simple rule of thumb is to search for strong firms that sell per share at less than twice their book value. NYSE Euronext (yes, it is the stock market itself), with a price-to-book-value ratio of 0.94, is an indicator of high value (at least as of May 2009).

Socially Responsible Investing

In recent years, socially responsible investment has also become prominent. This practice sees individuals invested only in firms that reflect their specific beliefs. For their "don'ts" as well as their "dos," socially conscious businesses are also selected. Such organizations should not manufacture cigarette products, drugs, guns, or items that are environmentally destructive.

Penny Stocks

Penny stocks are stocks that trade for $5 or less, and whether they're worth that much, you're fortunate in certain situations. Many penny stocks typically have no noticeable sales or dividends. For penny stocks, you have a strong chance for damages. Take time out to track the stock to see whether it has made some improvement if you have a deep desire to invest in this form of company. Learn what you can about the company, and don't be tempted to behave on a hot tip that your way might have been transferred.

Pink Sheets

In the pink sheets, a website run by the National Quotation Office, or on the NASDAQ small-cap exchange, Penny stocks trade. In short, pink sheets are listings and pricing details simply written on pink paper sheets that go to pick brokers.

Companies are poorly capitalized behind these stocks and are therefore not allowed to file reports with the SEC. They sell over the counter because there is a small range of accessible public knowledge. This is cause for alarm in itself. How many astute investors would like to bring their capital into an investment that provides little or no data? Nevertheless, individuals make a trade-in these stocks.

One of the most fascinating and disturbing facets of working with penny stocks is that brokers do not always act as a third party but instead fix rates and act as the transaction's principal. Most of the time, penny stocks do not have a standard premium, rather a range of various rates at which they may be bought or sold.

Chapter 2: Entering the stock market field

The stock market is one of the most exciting fields of investment. There are thousands of stocks from all over the world available for trading. There are stocks available for all budgets. There are stocks that only cost a few dollars per share and some high-end stocks worth thousands of dollars per share.

Stock trading is a massive industry where billions of dollars are traded every day. People from all walks of life are investing in stocks in the hopes that they will increase in value. Some people work with short sales or other options that focus on the market, falling in value. The diversity of the market is one of its most significants benefits, and there is something to interest everyone.

It takes an expert to know how to play the stock market and do well. Only the best and most seasoned traders can consistently find stocks that will be more likely to perform to their best potential.

This guide is to explain how the stock market works and how you can identify stocks of value.

What Makes Stocks and Options Different?

Stock trading and options are among the best investment opportunities. Many brokerage firms offer both of these services for investors. What are the distinctions between these two investment opportunities?

A stock is a fraction of ownership in a particular company - how much of something you own at a given time. You could hold as many shares of stock in a company as you can afford.

An option is not an actual form of ownership but rather a right to own or trade a certain investment. With an option, you have the right to buy or sell a particular stock at a certain value within a specific time period.

Intrinsic and Derivative Values

A stock's intrinsic value refers to the actual value of an asset or company. The value relates to how much confidence people have in a company and how well that group is growing. It might also change in value due to news stories or other reports surrounding the stock.

An option is based on the derivative value - the value of the security at a specific time. The price of a stock influences an option's value and simply adapts to the changes in the stock.

Long or Short-Term?

Regarding how long you have to hold an option or stock, there are no real rules. However, options have an expiry date. That is, an option will have to be exercised within a given time. You can set the specific time period at which the option will expire, thus allowing you to execute a purchase or sale at a certain value at that time period. You can keep an option running for as long as you want. Some options last for an hour. Others could go on for

a few days or even a few weeks. Knowing how to choose the right timing for an option is vital to your strategy.

Stocks are different in that you could hold them for as long as you deem necessary. Day-traders often trade stocks many times in the course of a day. This is interesting when you consider the potential for a stock to increase in value over the long-term. For instance, the Home Depot

(NYSE: HD) had its stock trading at around $80 during the start of 2014. As of February 2018, that stock has a value of a little more than $185.

Day-traders still benefit from changes in the value of a stock within a day. In a typical day, the same Home Depot stock could start at $185 and then move up to $188, down to $186, and then back to $188 at the end of the day.

Sensible Strategies

Create a strategy that you can use for your trades. Your strategy may be based on factors like:

- How you will enter into a trade

- How you will get out of that trade

- The total risk you have in each trade

- An analysis of how well a stock is performing

As you will discover throughout this guide, your plans for doing well in stock market investing should include multiple strategies in your trading plans based on what you find out based on your research and general common sense.

Online Resources

You will need to use quality online resources to help you manage your trades. There are various trading platforms that will help you identify what stocks are available will help you to execute trades and ones that list all the details about how a stock is moving. Historical information should be provided to you through one of these resources.

A stock screener is also vital to your investing success. This helps you have information on stocks based on specific criteria. You just add individual parameters into the program, and it would then find choices that fit.

Proper Education

Although you are not required to hold a degree to trade on the market, you must have the proper training. It is best to take advantage of an online program that teaches you about what is available and how to make trades.

Of course, if you are reading this guide, then the odds are you already understand the many points relating to online trades. There are various online trading schools that could give you information about how the market works. Groups like the Online Trading Academy, TradePro Academy, the Stock

Whisper, the Day-Trading Academy, Winner's Edge Trading, and many other groups have their own online programs. Even those who know about trading can still use these programs to clear up any confusion, one might have about how to trade properly. You can use them to practice the strategies that you will read about throughout this guide.

A Strong Mindset

The most important thing you need for day-trading is a good mindset. You need to be mentally prepared to trade and to accept what might occur, and be ready to respond immediately when something unexpected happens. Whether it is the price suddenly dipping or an option coming at the right time, you have to know when to play the market and when to stay out of it. You must also have a mindset that focuses on a strategy and staying with it throughout the entire investment process. When you are trading it is easy to lose track of what you are doing. You might come across several profitable trades that you did not expect to see, and you might not be fully prepared to execute those trades. Even worse, you might feel a desire to abandon a strategy because it is not working now and again. Do not veer from your strategy. Being persistent and clear of mind is vital to helping you stay focused.

Chapter 3: How to tell which stock is right for you?

It is incredible how many stocks are available, and you can easily find stocks in any field from any part of the world. The first strategy is knowing what stocks to invest in. Knowing how to pick a stock is essential. When deciding what stocks might be best for you, there are many points to consider. These points are vital to review regardless of the strategies you plan on using to invest.

Choose Stocks in a Field You Understand

The first tip for finding stock is to look for information on stocks in a field that you have actual knowledge about. It is easier to invest in stocks when you know about the market that stock is in, the factors that drive that market, and the competition that stock of interest might be encountering.

Regarding Home Depot, you might know that the stock is driven by the construction and home improvement industries. You would also know that the market features a competition with Lowe's, True Value, Home Hardware, and many other companies in the United States and Canada. Investigate Home Depot and the competition. Your knowledge of the business will help you feel more confident in the stock you choose.

The National Market

The New York Stock Exchange and NASDAQ make up the vast

majority of the world's trading volume. That does not mean you have to limit yourself to those two exchanges. You can also trade stocks from different exchanges throughout the world. These include the Japan Stock Exchange, Shanghai Stock Exchange, Euronext, and the London Stock Exchange. Additionally, the economy in one country might be radically different from another. For instance, there could be a bull market in Canada where the TMX Group exchange is based or in Germany where people trade on the Deutsche Borse. Meanwhile, India's bear market might cause the Bombay Stock Exchange and National Stock Exchange of India to fall in value. Therefore, it is best to stay with stocks based on exchanges with which you are familiar. You would have to research markets outside of the NYSE or NASDAQ. Just because an American stock is doing well does not mean that every other exchange in the world is going to perform the same. American markets are easier to analyze.

Do You Know the Company?

You have to investigate the company that you want to invest in. This includes knowing the following:

- what is the structure of the company in the past?
- Where is it based right now?
- The industry of the company.
- Any competitors of that company.

Updates on what that company is doing; this includes major news stories.

For instance, let's look at Sandridge Energy, Inc. (NYSE: SD). Do you know anything about SandRidge? The odds are you might not be familiar with the company unless you know about the natural gas and petroleum industry or if you live near the company's headquarters in Oklahoma City.

You might know more about Yum! Brands, Inc. (NYSE: YUM). This company is an organization that operates the KFC, Pizza Hut, and Taco Bell fast-food restaurants. You might have better access to information on what Yum! The brand is doing because the organization itself is so popular throughout the world.

You have the option to invest in companies that you are not familiar with. You should complete as much research on that business as possible, including how the business operates and how it has evolved over the years. Check that business's website and read its financial reports. Make sure you have enough information and that you are not struggling to find data on the stock. Getting as much knowledge about a company as possible is critical to your trading success.

Review Price Trends

The next thing to consider is how the value of a stock is trending. Every stock has its own trend as to how it goes up or down over time.

An example of noticing is how Sears Holdings (NASDAQ: SHLD) has been experiencing a downward trend in its stock over the years. Sears Holdings experienced a positive rise in its stock value in 2004 as the stock went from $20 to $110 over the course of a year. Soon after, the stock declined to $80 in 2006. The stock was trading around $20 during the late part of 2015. The value had been declining ever since and even fell below the $5 mark two years later.

Price trends can be helpful, but you should note how long those trends have been happening and if there have been any notable changes. The case of Sears Holdings is just one of many examples of how price trends can change. If a stock is declining in value does not mean it is going to keep moving down. The stock might move back up. It could happen due to positive economic reports or better market sentiment among investors.

Work With Moving Averages

A good idea for reviewing price trends is to take a look at the moving average of a stock. This refers to a series of averages of a stock's price over an extended period of time.

For instance, you might establish a 14-day moving average to see how the value of a stock is changing. This requires the following:

1. Take the closing price of a stock from each of the last 14 days.

2. Add all 14 of those closing prices together.

3. Divide that total by 14.

4. This will give you the full moving average.

5. Produce as many moving averages for 14-day spans as possible. For instance, you might compare the moving average for March 1-14 with the average for March 2-15, March 3-16, and so forth.

Using as many moving averages as possible, you can get an idea of how the value of stock changes. Day-traders benefit from shorter moving averages. You should use a variety of short and long-term averages if possible. This would give you an idea of how the market and individual stock values are changing. Looking at how a stock might shift in a short period of time is vital to your trading success, especially if you are trying to make brief trades as a day-trader.

The Relationship between Revenue and Debt

Revenues and debts are self-explanatory. These details can be found on the official SEC reports for a stock.

A business that is achieving more revenue will be doing more business. It would have enough funds to pay its employees, manage various operations, and cover some of the expenses or debts. Although the revenues of a business are vital, the debts that it holds might be overwhelming. These include costs for buying new assets, loans, or managing the salaries of various employees. Debts could be recurring, such as regular payments for loans and interest payments. They may also be one-time payments for assets needed for operational requirements. A business that has a lot of debt will be dangerous to invest in. This could be a significant threat that keeps a business from focusing on its overall growth.

Notice the gap between debts and revenues and how it has changed over time. Financial documents from a company should reveal what has influenced those totals and how they might expect to continue to change.

Compare the Performance of a Stock With Other Similar Choices

The next tip is to investigate how other stocks similar to what you want to invest in are doing. This gives you an idea of how well a stock is performing and if it is very different from others in the same market.

Let's say that you were looking at the stock in Macy's (NYSE: M). You might notice on a chart that Macy's stock is rising up and down in value with no real long-term trend evident. Look at other stocks in the same retail field to see if Macy's is a good stock to invest in. You might look for information on Kohl's (NYSE: KSS) and see that Kohl's stock has been steadily rising in value. Maybe Kohl's might be a better stock to invest in because of its performance.

Check multiple stocks in the same field. If you are going to work with a retail stock, check four or more retail-oriented stocks to see which one is developing the best. Review the backgrounds of these companies to see what makes these groups profitable or functional.

What is Best for Short or Long-Term Needs?

Take a look at the trends produced by certain stocks. How long are those trends been occurring? Maybe a stock is declining quickly like Sears, or it is volatile like the Home Depot. An extremely volatile stock would be better suited for day-trading purposes. The Home Depot stock might be worthwhile for day-trading because that stock fluctuates daily in value.

Meanwhile, a stock that has a long-term trend could be better to hold onto. Is the stock you are interested in gradually rising in value without experiencing much resistance? Is that stock not at risk of experiencing any substantial declines in the future? If so, you might want to invest in that stock and hold onto it for the foreseeable future. It will take months or even years to realize the best profits, but it will probably be worthwhile.

Signs a Stock is Better for Day-Trading

You do not have to day-trade every trade you complete. You can take a few stocks that are bound to rise in value over time and hold onto them for months. You should consider the following points if a stock that might be better for day-trading or at least for maintaining for just a few days at a time:

- A stock with a daily volume of 1 million or greater.

When the volume is high, the stock will be more likely to change in value. It could experience significant gains in just a few minutes.

- Stocks that are higher in value.

The potential for a big profit is greater when you trade a high-value stock. A stock with a value of $200 per share might change in value by $10 to $20 in a few hours. Something that is only $20 per share might move by just a few dollars at a time.

- Stocks that are extremely volatile.

A stock whose value changes from 1 to 5 percent in a day is better for day-trading. A stock with a higher volatility rate might change in value too dramatically; you must be ready to complete trades like this.

- You are not overly concerned about the background of the company.

Although it helps to research how well a company is operating and what it does, you might only have that company's stock for just a few minutes or hours. You do not necessarily have to perform a lot of research at this point (you should still do some research).

Signs a Stock Works for Long-Term Investing

We are going to talk about the other end of the trading spectrum. This listing entails signs that you should invest in a stock for months rather than just a few hours:

- It is easy for you to explain to people how a company makes money.

For instance, you could say that you know Kohl's or Macy's makes its money by selling consumer goods and fashions to other people. Any business that you understand and can explain easily is worthwhile.

- A company does not need much leverage for it to stay operational.

Look at the expenses that a company has to have to stay operational. Maybe a company has to spend a lot of money on machines and resources. In other cases, a company just buys from suppliers and sells those items. Whatever the case, discover what it takes for a business to operate and if it does not have much leverage to work with. Any business that does not require a lot of leverage might be easier to trust.

- A company has some kind of product or service that offers a distinct advantage.

Macy's offers popular high-end brands from many in-house and international vendors. Kohl's offers numerous reward programs for its customers. Sears has not only clothes but also appliances and even car maintenance services. All three of these retail companies are different, but they all have individual things about them that make them special. More importantly, those distinct features make a business stay afloat and competitive.

- The trend of a stock is consistent and does not look like it is going to change anytime soon.

The most important sign is how well the trend for a stock is working over the long-term. Look at several moving averages from the past few weeks to see how well a stock is performing. For instance, you can review the price of a stock for the past 10 to 15 Fridays. This reveals how the stock's value has evolved. A stock might be worth investing in if you find that the moving average has been going up consistently. Anything that keeps on increasing is a good bet.

The best stocks out there are always the ones that are easy to figure out and understand while having trends that are fully understandable.

Chapter 4: Reviewing an SEC report of a company for better stock investment.

One of the best ways to learn about what stocks to invest in is by looking at the official SEC reports that various company's issue. Any public company that has a stock must release one of these reports every year.

How a stock's data is laid out in an SEC report is one of the best strategies you can use for finding good stocks to invest in. As you look at this data, you have to identify many specifics in the report.

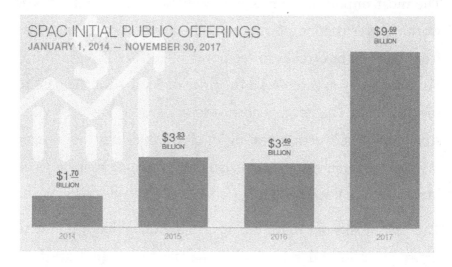

Background of a Report

To see why an SEC report is so important to incorporate into your trading research efforts, you need to see just why such reports exist in the first place. An SEC report is a document that a publicly-traded company must send out to the United States

Securities and Exchange Commission. These reports have been required since 1933, when the Securities Act was passed after the great stock market crash a few years earlier. The American government passed this to ensure all financial reports from publicly-traded companies were transparent and specific. This allows investors to make sensible decisions about what they want to invest in. This would discourage them from making stock purchases that they do not fully understand, a problem that caused the stock market crash of 1929 to occur in the first place.

Having a business share all its information with the public ensures that fraudulent activities will not be as likely to occur. Every business that you might want to invest in should have a proper SEC report available. The company's report should be detailed and provide many documents to prove the worth and operations of the company. Any business that fails to give enough SEC information might be suspect.

10-K Report

The first part of an SEC report to look at is the 10-K report. This is a basic document that gives a full summary of a company's performance. It is different from the report that a business gives to its shareholders in that the 10-K report does not provide any electoral processes.

This document is vital to understanding how a business works. It lets you see how the company is running and its various holdings and details. The comprehensive information is valuable. In fact, the 10-K report is the one thing that you should analyze above all others when looking at the SEC report. It showcases the basics you need to know to make your investment worthwhile.

Summary of Operations

The first point in the 10-K report to look at involves the summary of operations. This includes:

1. The business' background

The business's background provides information about what it does. For instance, the 10-k report for Apple (NASDAQ: AAPL) states that the technology company focuses on making consumer products like software, networking items, media players, and more.

2. The business' strategy

The strategy includes how the business is moving forward. In Apple's case, the strategy is to design new products and services within its own tech platform. This includes working with an extensive assortment of third-party development programs, among other features.

3. Information on current offerings

The offerings must include both the physical and non-physical items a company has. Apple's 10-k report has details on the various products, like the iPhone and iPad. It also reports on services and software programs like the iOS operating system software and the iCloud cloud storage service. General services provided. The 10-k report also provides details on what a company is providing outside of its products. Apple's 10k report says that it offers an extensive customer service team located in the United States and a few other call centers in different parts of the world.

4. Competition points

The 10-k report does not have to name any particular competitors. It should still include information on how other parties in the same field might offer certain products or services. Information on what a company is doing to try and make itself competitive or distinct from others could be found in the report as well.

5. Research and development data

The research and development section should include what a business is doing to find new products and make them available. Information on how much money a company is spending on R&D functions can be included. Apple's 10-k report shows that it spent almost twice as much on R&D operations in 2013 as what it spent in 2011.

6. Licenses, patents, copyrights, and trademarks

Any new applications for these legal markers can be included. This shows how committed a company is to what it is offering and prepared for any legal issues that might occur. You could benefit from investing in a company that cares about its efforts. Do not expect this section to be overly detailed. The company only has to list how it is acquiring legal protection to cover any applications that were sent out regardless of whether they have been fully accepted or not.

7. Foreign information

The foreign data refers to its operations outside of its base country. Apple lists in its 10-k report that it has outsourcing partners around Asia as well as a few other groups around North America and Europe. Apple lists this to let people know that the company has a foreign presence both for where it sells items and where its products are made.

8. Business seasonality

The seasonality report has details on when a company does much of its business. Apple says that a large portion of its sales occurs during the first quarter of that business' operation. This is around the Christmas season when Apple sells a large number of products that are intended to be gifted.

You can use this point in the 10-k report to strategize when you want to invest. You might have more luck investing in Apple during that company's first-quarter because it is a time when the business is growing and thriving.

Financial Outlook Information

The next part of the 10-k report involves the financial approaches that a company is using. The financial data should be listed under a section that reads "Selected Financial Data." The information can include the following:

- The net revenue from the business' operations

- The gross margin

- Costs for research and development

- Operating income

- The effective tax rate that a business is working with

- The total value of the assets that a business has the debt held by the business.

How many employees a business has; might explain part of why expenses might start to rise in some cases

The financial information should include historical points as well. Take the 10-k report that Intel (NASDAQ: INTC) has released to the public. This includes information on the net revenue for the company from 2007 to 2016. The report shows that Intel had nearly $60 billion in revenue in 2016. That total was $35 billion in 2009, increasing to $52 billion in 2013. Getting historical information is important to understand how well a business is developing and how its finances have changed. The financial outlook must be as thorough as possible to know whether or not something is a suitable choice for your investment.

Balance Sheet

The next section of the 10-k report is the balance sheet. This should be listed near the "Financial Statements and Supplementary Data" section of the report. The sheet must include the following information:

1. The assets of the company

These can include short and long-term assets. Such assets can include cash, inventory, accounts receivable, and other investments. They should also include equipment or properties that a business holds.

2. The liabilities of the business

Short-term liabilities are orders that might be coming occurring right now. Customer advances account payable, and any taxes or interest that a business owes should be included. Long-term liabilities are debts. These include debts for bonds payable or any lengthy loans that have to be paid off. The short and long-term debts should be divided into their own sections in this listing of information.

3. The shareholders' equity

This refers to the assets minus the liabilities. It is a basic measurement of how healthy a company is. The total focuses on what might be returned to shareholders if the company's assets were liquidated and its debts were paid off. A business whose equity total is increasing is always worth investing in as that company stock has a better chance to increase in value.

This section should include information on both the preferred and current stock that is associated with a company. Preferred stock is for those who get more dividends and might have more access to certain company assets. Common stock includes voting rights for major decisions that a business will make. (Note: A majority of the stocks you will find on the market are common stock; preferred stock typically is offered to people within a business).

These three points are vital to be included on the balance sheet. There are a few strategies you can use to help you decide whether or not to invest in a company:

- Focus on the current assets. These are the assets that can be converted into cash.

Looking at the current assets helps you discover why a business's finances might have changed in recent times and if there has been a significant influx of sales or contracts.

- Are the non-current assets intangible?

Intangible assets include the general reputation and goodwill that a business holds. A company like Intel or Apple might have a significant amount of goodwill because they have produced various products for many people, and each has a devoted fan base.

- Watch for the depreciation that might get in the way of investment.

The depreciation here refers to the times when the investment shrinks in value. Physical equipment or goods can depreciate over time, causing the total value of assets to decline.

- Review how long the long-term debts might exist.

Some long-term debts could include loans that might exist for ten years or more. Others might expire in a year, thus giving a business a bit of freedom for what it can handle from an investment standpoint.

- Calculate the debt ratio.

The debt ratio can be utilized to help you figure out how much an investment is worth. Take the total debt and divide it by the total assets. For instance, a business with $15 million in debts might have $25 million in assets. The debt ratio here would be 0.6. That is, the assets outweigh the debts.

What if those numbers were reversed? A business with $25 million in debt and $15 million in assets would have a debt ratio of 1.666.

A business with a greater debt ratio will surely be dangerous to consider investing in. This type of business would be in real trouble because it does not have enough assets. You should still look at why the business attained so many debts just to discover what is going on in the business.

Income Statement

The income statement is a good document to read when deciding on your strategy for investing. The income statement refers to the data that covers what a business is earning overtime.

The statement should include information for at least the last three years of business. Anything more with background data helps to give you a clearer idea of where a business is going and if it has had any new expenses over the years.

The income statement should include the following details:

1. The total revenue

2. The cost of the revenue

The difference between these two points is the gross profit or gross loss.

1. Operating expenses

These expenses may include research and development, general administrative costs, and any possible non-recurring expenses.

Subtract the operating expenses from the gross profit to get the total operating income or loss.

2. Income from ongoing operations

This income is what a company earns before interest and taxes.

3. Interest and tax expenses

Depreciation costs may be included in this section or at least documented on a separate line.

Subtract the interest and tax from the income to determine the net income.

Focus your strategies on businesses that are earning enough income versus the expenses it has. Taxes might be higher in value as a company makes more money, but that is just a natural progression of how a business develops. The tax expenses might vary based on where a company is incorporated. This might influence the report as a business might be in some part of the world where taxes are minimal or nonexistent. The 10-k report should tell you at the start if the business is incorporated in some place outside of where it is based, so you at least know why tax expenses might not be significant.

Cash Flow Report

The cash flow report analyzes the cash flow, a measurement of how much money is being moved in and out of business. It is a symbol of liquidity as it measures how well a business can keep its operations afloat. It lets you know if a business is making the right choices to pay off debts, managing its inventory, or even its R&D functions.

The cash flow report offers more information on what is happening in a business than an income statement. The problem with an income statement is that it just focuses on cash-related items. The cash flow report incorporates every asset and feature in the statement giving you a better idea of what a business's assets and position are in reality. That does not mean you should ignore the income statement; both of these statements are critical to understanding if you should invest or not. The cash flow report should include:

1. The net earnings of the business

2. The operating cash flow

The cash flow refers to the money that has been spent over a period of time or what that business has earned. This may include details on sales from the credit, expenses for paying creditors, and so forth. A cash flow report should include specific reasons why the cash flow is where it is. This could consist of increases in accounts payable and decreases in accounts receivable.

Naturally, you will want to consider a company that has a slightly larger cash flow. There are times when a company might have a negative cash flow as more money is moving out of the business.

1. The asset investments being utilized

The cash that was used to sell or buy significant assets can be listed here. It could include details on equipment, machines, furniture, securities, insurance plans, or anything else being used at a time. A business that spends more on its investments might have a lower cash flow, but that business aims to grow. Those new investments may be used for future profits and to make things within a business more productive or otherwise proficient.

Some companies will spend more money on investments or at least reserve some of their funds for future use. This is especially the case for tech stocks. Tech companies often reserve massive amounts of money for possible innovations or for any anticipated future demands that they anticipate happening.

2. Money received or paid through financing

The money received from or paid to creditors and investors should be listed. The sales of stocks or bonds may be included. Dividend stocks should list details on how dividends were paid out. Some companies might buy back their stocks if necessary.

This section of the 10-k report is vital in that it focuses heavily on how the business could grow. There are many factors that will directly cause a stock's cash flow to increase:

- Extra sales

- Getting new contracts with other businesses or groups for long-term sales

- Selling equipment

- Selling off shares or other investments

Any investments having grown before being sold off; these include any resources the business has a decrease in the cash flow could occur due to a variety of issues:

- Employee salaries having to be paid out

- Buying new resources or equipment

- Paying for repairs for equipment and maintenance

- Paying out dividends to investors

- Lawsuits or other forms of litigation; any value of legal issues might be factored into the losses

This is only a small listing of the decreases and increases you might encounter when searching for an investment.

There are a few extra tips to use when looking at a cash flow report:

- While a positive cash flow is always good, it is even better when the cash flow comes from operations.

When the money is from operations, it suggests that the company is generating enough business and acquiring more inventory or new pieces of equipment. A company that has less than half of its cash coming from operations might be too risky to invest in.

- Has a business expanded its operations?

A business with a negative cash flow might be in the middle of an expansion project. This means that the business is trying to grow and needs to spend extra to handle the expansion. See what has caused the flow to decline.

- Look at the length of the loans.

Loans can be arranged for years before they are due. Sometimes a loan might be paid off sooner. Review how the loans are being paid and for how long.

To understand the importance of cash flow, you need to look at the example of WorldCom. The company's stock fell apart in the 2000s in a dramatic fashion. Many people saw WorldCom had a sizable amount of income growth, but they ignored to the cash flow. The investors did not know that WorldCom had a very poor cash flow and was significantly smaller than the net income. WorldCom was not investing and had been losing money despite all their income growth. Any investor who noticed that WorldCom's cash flow was poor could have made the smart move and decide not to actually invest in the stock. Considering how WorldCom fell apart, staying away would have surely been the best bet.

Legal Proceedings

The legal proceedings of a report are vital to analyzing. This refers to the lawsuits or other complicated court proceedings that a business is experiencing. These are events that are outside standard litigation.

Let's go back to the Apple 10-k report. Apple reported information on a few legal cases it experienced in its 2013 report. It included information on Apple losing nearly $370 million in a 2010 case against a company that claimed Apple infringed upon certain patents. A 2012 case where Apple was rewarded about $1 billion from another suit was also included.

The legal proceedings section should include details on the official names of the court cases involved and how much money they were worth regardless of who the court favored. Information on why litigation was instigated should be included as well.

You might want to look for additional information on any legal proceedings of a company by researching the cases on the websites of the groups that heard those cases. For instance, a case heard by the United States Department of Justice can be researched online at **www.justice.gov.** This site will give you full information on court proceedings and the background data surrounding those cases.

A company should be straightforward and direct about its legal proceedings in this part of a 10-k report. A company that is willing to give as much information on these proceedings as possible is always easier to trust because that company is not afraid to acknowledge some of the concerns it might have. You should still look at those outside websites as a business might still try to hide information about its legal issues.

Risk Factors

The 10-k report identifies the risk factors that a business face. These factors include concerns that a business feels will directly impact its future earnings. Think of it as the W part of a SWOT analysis.

Intel's 10-k report lists numerous risk factors that could hurt the business. The report reveals how it is difficult for the company to predict the demand for its products. It also mentions how Intel faces a sizable competition and is also subjected to many variables in international markets that could directly make a difference in how well the company can earn revenue and keep itself operational.

The risks listed here can include both problems relating to the outside market and also within the business itself. Intel states that it is at risk of product defects or errors that might impact its products. This risk could result in recalls or significant expenses, not to mention the potential for Intel's reputation to be damaged.

These points on the 10-k report are vital for you to analyze when deciding what stocks you should invest in. Check the entire report before you execute a trade to understand where a business is going and how it might potentially change in value.

10-Q Report

A 10-q report is similar to a 10-k report but concentrates on the quarterly work of a business.

Let's look at a 10-q report that the Coca-Cola Company (NYSE: KO) listed in July 2017. This was for financial information during the quarter from April to June 2017.

Coca-Cola's 10-q report included a series of important things:

1. Financial statements surrounding gross profits, operating income, taxes, and various expenses

Many of the financial points highlighted in the 10-q report are identical to what a 10-k report features. This just gives a better idea of what a company has done recently.

2. Details on any significant developments that took place in the past quarter

Coca-Cola listed on its 10-q report that it acquired a plant-based beverage company and also franchised some of its operations in China.

3. Contracts set up with other groups

These contracts may be agreements for services and products from various groups and deals between individual people at a given time.

4. Ongoing legal proceedings and risk factors

In most cases, you might refer back to the last 10-k form a company released. This is for cases where nothing new has happened in the market.

Updates on any legal cases that are still unresolved can be included too.

8-k Report

The 8-k report is also known as the Current Report. This is issued by companies when they have major events that they need to let the public know about. Sometimes the report is about something that causes a company to grow in size. In other cases, the report is about some difficult problems that might be red flags for your investment strategy. An 8-k report can be filed to discuss any of the following:

- Issuing bankruptcy
- Entering into or leaving a material definitive agreement
- The completion of a major acquisition plan
- Any events that cause a financial obligation to change

Cases where estimates that a business is expected to earn are dramatically altered in value; this is usually when the value of something decreases

- Amendments to the company Code of Ethics
- The introduction of key issues and developments that shareholders will have to vote on

An example of this is the 8-k report Coca-Cola Company released in mid-February 2018. The company issued an 8-k report stating that the company experienced great operating results during the fourth quarter of the prior fiscal year. The report included information on all the financial developments that took place at the time. Coca-Cola sent out an 8-k report in December 2017 stating that a major member of the company board was departing. Another report from the same company in October 2017 said that the company had good third-quarter results.

There are no limits as to how many 8-k reports a business can send out. You would have to look at how these are listed. A company should be very thorough and transparent when publishing these reports, so people will understand what is causing a company to change in some way.

Internal Functions

SEC filings should include details on all the internal functions that a business is experiencing. This includes a full description of how the business is operated and who is in charge, as well as any suspicious actions that those people are engaging in. There are three specific documents to look into when reviewing the internal functions of a business.

Proxy Statement

The proxy statement refers to management information and filings made by the company. It must be filed before an annual meeting where shareholders may vote on functions that take place within the business. The report gives you an idea of how the management of the business operates and how people involved might get paid. It also lists possible conflict of interest concerns that people might have with certain auditors.

To understand how a proxy statement works, let's look at the statement that Southwest Airlines (NYSE: LUV) released in April 2017. The following points were included in the statement:

- Information on how people can enter into the voting process.

- How voting procedures work?

- Details of the people involved and any conflicts of interest they might have.

The Southwest Airlines proxy statement said that various Board Members should continue to hold their positions because of multiple factors relating to experience and skills. Each person was listed citing their educational background, prior jobs in the aviation field, and so forth.

- Information on how executives were compensated

Southwest listed information on special bonuses that executives could get based on certain performance thresholds. These include how many sales were managed at a given time. Incentives for performance and bonuses should be listed in a proxy statement. Deferred compensation may also be included, as well as any perks like private vehicle access or special travel services.

- Auditing functions

The listing of who is on the auditing committee was listed to identify how the auditing process within the business would be organized.

You can find proxy statements for businesses by doing the following:

1. Go to the SEC website and review its EDGAR database.

2. Enter in the particular business for which you want information.

3. Look for a filing that has the DEF 14A title. This gets its name for being the definitive proxy statement in accordance with Section 14(a) of the Securities Exchange Act.

What makes the proxy statement important? The proxy statement is vital for a business to inform shareholders about the executive functions in the workplace. It lets people know that a business has a sensible plan for when certain decisions have to be made that might influence the direction that the business will have in the future.

You should consider investing in businesses that have transparent and direct proxy statements. Such businesses are often easier to trust because they want people to understand the workings of their operation.

Schedule 13D

Schedule 13D is a part of SEC filings that covers details on who owns shares. A company must file it within ten days after a person acquires 5 percent or more of any security. This provides information on how one person may be managing much of the company's shares. It could be a sign that a business might be heavily influenced by one person. The Schedule 13D report must include the following:

- Details on the security

- Information on the person who acquired the security

This should include a person's contact information and background. Any criminal records of that person should be listed if applicable.

- The source of the funds for the transaction

Sometimes the money comes from leveraged or borrowed funds. A transaction that uses money the investor actually has full control over is always better.

- The reason why someone is acquiring these shares; is also called the Purpose of Transaction

This could be because an investor is heavily interested in a certain company and feels that the stock is undervalued. It could also be a sign of someone trying to acquire a sizable portion of the company. Even those who are trying to enter into a hostile takeover should be listed here.

- Any contracts or relationships that the investor has with other people within the business

- Letters and other documents that express how the transaction occurred

The Schedule 13D form is part of the SEC filing that should be reviewed for details and to ascertain if someone wants to acquire a significant number of shares.

Form 144

Form 144 covers how stocks are made available to the public. Form 144 must be filed when someone associated with the company plans on selling stock. This includes a Director, Executive, or another figure.

Form 144 is a simple two-page document. It must be filled out with the following details:

- The name of the issuer of the stock

- The title of the class of securities that will be sold

- The number of shares that will be sold

- The market value of those shares

- How many shares are outstanding?

- When the shares are expected to be sold

- The names of the securities exchanges being used at a given time Information on any other securities that the person selling the shares might have sold in the past three months.

Form 144 should factor into your investment strategy as you look at how shares are being made available to the public. Sometimes a Form 144 report is a sign that someone in a business wants to retire and is going to sell off their shares. In other cases, it might be a sign that something major is going to take place in the business, like someone else buying out part of that entity.

Added Tips

Everything that goes into a company's SEC reports will give you a good idea of how a business is run and what makes it outstanding or distinct. While the information listed is worthwhile, there are many intricate parts of an SEC report that you should delve into as well. These features tell more about the stock and can help you formulate your strategies for investing.

Review the EPS

A valuable strategy to use is to watch for the EPS. This refers to the earnings per share of stock. Although a business does not actually have to declare this total in its SEC report, you can still figure this out easily:

1. Look for the net income that the report shows.

2. Divide that net income by the number of shares that investors hold.

3. This should give you an idea of how much money is involved in each share.

This is a good measurement of how well a business is doing. When the EPS is high, it means the business is growing and evolving. This could be a good time for you to invest, but you should still look at why the total is moving up as much as it is. Sometimes the EPS might be increasing because the business bought back some of its shares from others. The EPS might also go down because the business issued more shares. Whatever the case might be, you have to determine how the EPS is formed and why that total is where it is.

Don't Forget Assumptions

An EPS might include a series of assumptions by the business that produces the document. These are based on prior earnings, forecast totals, and general plans for the business as time moves along. Decide how realistic those assumptions might be. A business with a small growth rate of 1 to 2 percent might say that it has expectations to grow by 3 to 5 percent. This is sensible as it shows the business growing and being more visible. However, a business that claims it will experience an extremely high increase, such as from 2 percent to 15 percent growth, should be avoided as it seems unrealistic. Any business that does not add assumptions might not be thinking about the future. It might assume that certain functions are going to stay sluggish or lacking in some way.

Consider Economic Conditions

As you review the SEC report, think about the overall economic conditions of the business in question. Sometimes this might involve the entire economy. In other cases, it just involves a smaller segment of the economy. Consider how the economy is developing or not developing.

The net income or near earnings of a business should be compared with the sales revenue that the business receives. More importantly, it should be analyzed in the context of whatever the business environment might be like at a particular time. Sometimes the business climate is healthy, or it might be that it is difficult for a business to grow and develop.

Conditions within a region where a business operates might be a factor as well. An international organization might focus on one part of the world. For instance, Yum! Brands concentrate on the United States, Canada, United Kingdom, and China. Those four markets have their own individual economic climates. Reviewing the international factors surrounding a stock gives you an idea of how certain regions help or hinder a business. The gains that a business has in China might offset the losses in the United States, for instance.

Watch for One-Time Changes

When looking at the details on an SEC report, look carefully at some individual one-time changes that might take place as they could directly impact your investment.

There are many reasons why a huge one-time change might appear on a report:

- A business might have invested in some new pieces of equipment or inventory. These include totally new things that a business has never had a use for before. This could indicate a business trying to expand.

- It may also suggest that there is a lawsuit or other legal action that a business just experienced that might have resulted in a significant amount of money paid out due to a court struggle.

- An acquisition of another company might be the reason for the change.

Watch For Confusing or Vague Content

Another thing to consider when reviewing SEC reports is that many SEC reports might be confusing. They could contain lots of terms that you are not familiar with. Maybe the reports include documents that are vague or certain bits of information are not listed even though the SEC states that it should be listed. This is often a sign that a business is trying to hide something.

What If a New Version of a Report Is Issued?

Sometimes a business might issue a new version of an SEC report. The most common reason this happens is that a business has engaged in inaccurate accounting practices. Sometimes a business could have committed fraudulent accounting by intentionally lying about the finances.

Any company that issues a revision of an SEC report might not be trustworthy. Look for information on why the report was revised before you consider buying the stock.

What About the Chairman's Letter?

The Chairman's letter is a document in an SEC report that most people ignore. It is simply a message to the investors about what and how a business is doing.

There is much more to the letter than you may think. Reviewing the Chairman's letter is one of the best strategies you can utilize to discover the direction of a business. It all comes with firsthand knowledge of the business from the leader. When reading the letter, the Chairman should mention:

- The business's financial strengths and concerns are based on debt levels, cash flow, and other points.

- The challenges that the business is facing. These include problems relating to competition, issues within the business, or even the economy in general.

- Recent measures have been undertaken to make the business more financially viable regardless of whether they entail expansion or cost-cutting measures.

- The consistency of the business' strategy and if the strategy being used is slightly different from what it was a few years earlier.

The letter should be detailed and easy to understand. After all, the Chairman is the one whose job could be on the line depending on how well a business is performing.

Searching through SEC reports can be a challenge because they can be complicated and detailed. The more you review what is in an SEC report, the easier it will become for you to decide which company you could benefit from by making an investment.

Two Proven Ways to Analyze Stocks

Investors generally favor one of two stock-picking techniques: technical analysis or fundamental analysis. Technical analysis is all about stock prices and how they move, and it relies on charts and graphs to determine patterns. Fundamental analysis, more common among beginning investors, involves studying the company itself, with a focus on financial statements and performance. For optimum results, many savvy investors combine both techniques when making trade decisions. For example, a stock with great fundamentals and sagging price trends could indicate trouble on the horizon.

Technical analysis focuses on charts and graphs showing past stock price and volume patterns. There are a number of patterns technical analysts recognize to be historically recurring. The trick is to identify the pattern before it is completed, then buy or sell according to where the pattern indicates the stock is headed. Those who use this technique believe you can forecast future stock prices by studying past price trends. They make trades based primarily on stock price movements. Technical analysts tend to do much more buying and selling than fundamental analysts.

Fundamental analysis is a long-used, common way to review stocks. The technique involves an analysis of the company's ability to generate earnings and an examination of its total assets' values. Value investing and growth investing are two subdivisions of fundamental analysis. Proponents of fundamental analysis believe that stock prices will rise as a result of growth. Earnings, dividends, and book values are all examined, and a buy-and-hold approach is usually followed. Fundamental analysis advocates maintain that stock in well-run, high-quality companies will become more valuable over time.

Five Characteristics of Great Companies

Once you've narrowed your focus to a handful of companies, you need to fine-tune your research even more. One of the first reasons to buy a particular stock is because of its future outlook. It's wise to buy and hold onto a stock for the long term, so quality is an important part of your investment strategy. Among other factors, you want to purchase stock in a company that you believe has the following traits:

1. **Sound business model.** You want to single out a company that has a solid business plan and a good grasp of where it wants to be in the years ahead, and a plan to get there. A company with a clear focus has a better chance of reaching its goals and succeeding than a company that just rolls along without a concrete plan.

2. **Superior management.** An experienced, innovative, and progressive management team has the best chance of leading a company into the future. Star managers have had a major impact on their

prospective companies, and a company will often witness dramatic changes when a new management team comes onboard. When key management leaves an organization, you will often see major changes in the way a company operates.

3. **Significant market share.** When a majority of individuals rely upon the products and/or services of a designated company, odds are the company has good insight into consumer preferences. Industry market leaders usually have a well-thought-out vision. However, the strongest company performance doesn't always indicate the best stock to buy. Be careful and look more closely at markets with a glut of competitors; sometimes, the second-best company makes the best stock investment.

4. **Competitive advantages.** A company that is ahead of the pack will often be on top of cutting-edge trends and industry changes in areas like marketing and technology. You want to single out those companies that are—and are likely to stay— one step ahead of the competition.

5. **New developments.** If a company places a high priority on research and development, it's likely to roll out successful introductions. If the product or service takes off, the stock price may very well follow.

If the future outlook for a particular company appears promising— that is, as long as a company continues to exhibit these traits and act upon them—owning a portion of that company might make good business sense.

Chapter 5: Bonds

BONDS, MUTUAL FUNDS, AND ETFs

The sole method of investment is not individual stocks. There are several other items you can invest in, and shares, mutual funds, and exchange-traded funds are three of the most common (ETFs). It is both a matter of personal style and your tolerance for risk where you place your assets. For one, the value of mutual funds is that you're actually paying someone else to handle the money for you. On the other side, if you don't like ceding the power of your investments to anyone else, you might not think of it as a benefit. We will look at these three forms of investment in this chapter: their benefits and drawbacks.

WHAT ARE BONDS?

Loaning Money for Interest

Bonds are part of a completely different asset class than stocks. Like the stock market, the bond market is heavily influenced by global economic and political trends—but to a much higher degree. In fact, the world bond market is considerably larger and more influential than the stock market, and much of the world economy depends on international bond trading.

If interest rates rise:

Yields
Rise

Prices
Fall

If interest rates fall:

Prices
Rise

Yields
Fall

The Definition of Bonds

Bonds are marketable securities that represent a loan to a company, a municipality, the federal government, or a foreign government with the expectation that the loan will be paid back at a set date in the future (that is to say when the bond matures). Like almost all loans, bonds also come with an interest component, which can involve periodic payments over the life of the bond or single payments at maturity. Bonds can be bought directly as new government issues, from a municipality, or from a company. They can also be bought from bond traders, brokers, or dealers on the secondary market. The bond market dictates how easily you can buy or sell a bond and at what price.

Why Sell Bonds?

Governments, whether municipal, state, or federal, sell bonds for a very simple reason: to raise money. Usually, the money is for a specific project: building a bridge, repairing a road, etc. During the Second World War, the federal government sold bonds to raise money for the war effort.

A big part of the bond picture is interesting. For lending them the money, the borrower (or issuer of the bond) agrees to pay the buyer a specific rate of interest at predetermined intervals. Bonds are sold in discrete increments (typically multiples of $1,000, with few exceptions), known as their par value or face value. Bonds' maturities and interest rates vary:

- Short-term bonds mature in up to five years

- Intermediate-term bonds generally mature at seven to ten years Long-term bonds usually mature around twenty to thirty years

Longer-term bonds typically will pay higher interest rates—averaging higher than 6 percent over the last fifty years—than short-term bonds. Though the bond's stated interest rate is a known factor, over time, its yield (or effective interest rate) will fluctuate along with changes in prevailing interest rates; this matters primarily if you are trying to sell a bond.

Use Bonds to Diversify

Because bond values often move in the opposite direction of the stock market, bonds can help you diversify your portfolio, thus reducing risk. They are also an important part of asset allocation strategies essential for good portfolio management. While bonds typically don't function as a complete substitute for stocks, they do make a strong complement, in addition to providing you with steady interest income.

A bond will have a date of final maturity, which is when the bond will return your principal or initial investment. Some types of bonds—known as callable bonds—can be redeemed by the issuer earlier than that maturity date, which means that the lender pays you back sooner than expected. A $5,000 bond is worth $5,000 upon maturity (regardless of the price that bond would fetch on the open market), as long as the issuer does not default on the payment. The interest you receive while holding the bond is your perk, so to speak, for lending the money. Interest is usually paid semiannually or annually, and it compounds at different rates.

Bonds versus Stocks

Unlike a stockholder, a bondholder does not take part in the success or failure of the company. Shares of stock will rise and fall in conjunction with the company's fortunes. In the case of bonds, you will receive interest on your loan and get your principal back at the date of maturity regardless of how well a company fares—unless, of course, it goes bankrupt. Bonds are therefore referred to as fixed-income investments because you know how much you will earn— unless you sell before maturity, in which case the market determines the price.

Corporate bond prices, like stock prices, can be affected by corporate earnings. However, they are often affected to a much stronger degree by fluctuations in interest rates. This is true even though the bond market itself often takes the lead in setting those rates. And both types of securities are subject to influences like terrorism, politics, and fraud.

Seven Features

When you're considering a bond for your portfolio, remember to analyze these seven key features:

1. Price

2. Stated interest rate

3. Current yield

4. Maturity

5. Redemption features

6. Credit rating

7. Income tax impact

These factors can help you decide whether this bond fits into your portfolio and meshes with your personal investment goals.

Bond Risks

As a general rule, bonds, particularly U.S. government bonds, are considered less risky than stocks and are therefore considered a more conservative investment (government bonds are very low risk because there's little chance the government will go bankrupt). Bonds also tend to provide a higher rate of interest than you can get from a bank account or CD, and this, along with a steady flow of interest income, usually makes them attractive, relatively safe investments.

There are drawbacks and risks inherent to bonds. The most basic risk is that an issuer may default, meaning you will not get your money back. You can also lose money in bonds if you are forced to sell when interest rates are high. And you may not see the type of high returns from bond investments that you can realize from more risky equity mutual funds or from a hot stock.

WHY BUY BONDS?

Reduce Risk

Adding some bonds or bond mutual funds to your investment portfolio is a good idea, especially if you have a lower tolerance for risk. For investors of every kind, bonds offer a wide variety of benefits.

Two are especially important:

1. Bonds can help stabilize a portfolio by offsetting the investor's exposure to the volatility of the stock market. Bonds inherently have different risk and return character than stocks, so they will necessarily behave differently when the markets move.

2. Bonds generally provide a scheduled stream of interest payments (except zero-coupon bonds, which pay their interest at maturity). This attractive feature helps investors meet expected current income needs or specific future monetary needs, such as college tuition or retirement income.

Callable bonds and pass-through securities have less predictability, but investors are compensated for the uncertainty in the form of higher yields.

Unlike stocks, bonds are designed to return the original investment, or principal, to the investor at future maturity date.

This preservation of capital provides stability to your portfolio and balances the growth/risk aspect of stocks. You can still lose your principal investment if you sell your bonds before maturity at a price lower than your purchase price or if the borrower defaults on payment. By choosing high-credit-quality bonds, you can limit your exposure to default risk.

Another significant advantage: certain bonds provide unique tax benefits. For example, you won't be paying any state or local income tax on the interest you've earned on your U.S. Treasury bonds. Likewise, the interest on your municipal bonds (usually) won't be subject to a federal income tax bite, and in some cases, they'll be free of state or local income taxes, too. A good broker or tax advisor can help you determine which bonds are best for you.

The Risks Unique to Bonds

As is the case with all investments, there is some degree of risk involved in bond investing. Several types of risks pertain specifically to bonds. Here are three of the most significant risks and how they affect the bond market.

Call Risk

Among the less common risks in bonds, investments are call risk, which means the issuer can buy you out of your investment before maturity. That can happen when rates drop, and they want to call in high-interest bonds to issue new ones at the new lower rate. But situations like these are less common, especially in a period of stable or rising interest rates.

Credit Risk

This is the risk of default by the company issuing the bond, resulting in the loss of your principal investment. This is why bonds are rated, just like people looking for credit. Government bonds—at least in theory—don't have this risk and therefore need not be graded; they are simply safe investments. As a potential investor, you need to compare the risk and the yield, or return, you will get from different grades of bonds. If, for example, you will do almost as well with a high-grade tax-exempt municipal bond as you will do with a lower-grade taxable corporate bond, take the safer route and buy the municipal bond. Buying riskier bonds or lower-grade bonds is only worthwhile if you will potentially see returns big enough to merit taking that credit risk.

Interest-Rate Risk

If you are keeping a bond to maturity, interest-rate risk is not terribly significant since you will not be particularly affected by changing interest rates. However, if you are selling a bond, you need to concern yourself with the rate of interest that ties in with the yield of the bond. Essentially, the risk is that you will be stuck holding a long-term bond that pays less than the current interest rate, making it hard to sell and reinvest your capital.

Avoid Defensive Buying

Buy bonds based on your needs and financial situation.

Plan to buy a particular bond and hold it to maturity. Don't be intimidated by a broker who asks, "But what if you need to sell the bond?" Buying just in case you need to sell is defensive buying, and you may regret it in the long run.

The longer the maturity of the bond, the more a change in yield will affect the price. You will better manage interest-rate risk by buying shorter maturities and rolling them over. However, if you are looking for higher returns over a longer period of time, you should go with the longer-term bond and hope you do not have to sell it.

Many financial brokers talk a great deal about the interest fluctuations on bonds. This is because they are in the business of buying and selling them. Many bond owners, however, tuck bonds away for years and enjoy the income generated. Therefore, before worrying greatly about the interest-rate fluctuations making your bond more or less valuable in the secondary market, decide on your plan. Are you buying bonds to sell them or to hold them to maturity? If you consider yourself financially sound and are simply looking to purchase a long-term bond for a future goal, then, by all means, go with your plan. Since the idea is to hold onto the bond until it matures, you will enjoy the higher yield. Even if you are forced to sell fifteen-year bond twelve years toward maturity, and you take a loss on the price, you will have still enjoyed higher yields than you would have with short-term bonds.

Income Risk

This is a double risk: first, that should you sell, you won't get the full value (or par), and second that inflation will surpass the rate of income you are receiving from the bond (known as inflation risk). If you are reinvesting your interest income, you also will see less immediate income. However, you will be building your investments.

The best way to manage income risk is to stagger or ladder your bonds so that you can pick up the higher interest rates along the way. Inflation risk can be combated by simply re-evaluating your asset allocation and possibly moving to an investment that is higher than the inflation rate until it drops. If you already have an income-producing bond paying a rate of 3.9 percent, and inflation has gone up to 4.1 percent, you can reinvest the income in a higher-yield (perhaps slightly riskier) vehicle. An equity fund will more likely beat the inflation rate.

BOND RATINGS AND YIELDS

How Good Is a Bond?

Corporate bonds and some municipal bonds are rated by financial analysts at Standard & Poor's (S&P) and Moody's, among others. The ratings indicate the creditworthiness of the bond issuer and are, therefore, a report card of sorts on the company issuing the bond. Analysts look at the track record and financial situation of the company, the rate of income, and the degree of risk associated with the bond. All of this information is put together, and the bonds are graded. This is very similar to a personal credit rating, where people who are more likely to pay their debts in full and on time get higher scores than people who may not pay on time or at all.

- A rating or grade of AAA goes to the highest-quality bond. Bonds rated AAA, AA, A, or BBB (Aaa, Aa, A, or Bbb in Moody's system) are considered high quality. BB or B bonds are more questionable.
- Anything below B, such as C- or D-level bonds, are considered low-grade or junk bonds.

However, if you pick the right rising company, a junk or high-yield bond can be very successful. But the risks are high, especially the default risk.

How Do Bonds Pay Interest?

A fixed interest rate is the most common, although interest can be paid at a floating rate, which changes based on economic conditions. Zero-coupon bonds pay no ongoing interest. Instead, at a deep discount they are sold and at full value are redeemed, causing them to build up, through compounding interest, to their face value.

If you own corporate bonds that used to be solidly rated but have fallen on hard times, you have two choices: sell or hold. Part of your choice will be based on whether you believe the company will turn itself around and get back in the black; the other side of the decision is more immediately practical. If you don't believe the company will

ever be able to pay its debts, get out while you can; if you believe the company will pull through—and maybe even emerge stronger— consider keeping the bonds. When the bond is in your portfolio primarily for income purposes (i.e., regular interest payouts that you count on as income), and that income stream is still flowing, it can make sense to hold onto it. On the other hand, if the bond is used as a hedge against riskier stocks or to give you a big lump of cash down the line, consider selling right away before the bond price drops so low that you won't recoup a sizeable chunk of your investment.

Bond ratings for an issuer can change over time. A company issuing BBB bonds may become a much more stable fixture as a largely successful company, and their bonds may be A-rated next time they are graded. The opposite can happen as well: Highly rated corporations can fall on hard times and have their debt downgraded, sometimes substantially. It's a good idea to keep tabs on the grades of the bonds you own for the purpose of potential resale, as the grade does affect the bond's marketability.

Bond Yields

When it comes to bond investing, you need to know about the two types of yields: the yield to maturity and the current yield. They absolutely affect how much your bonds are worth on the open market.

One of the most (if not the most) important factors in determining bond yields, and therefore bond prices, is the prevailing interest rate. Essentially, the stated interest rate on your bond will be compared to the current interest rate for equivalent debt instruments. Whether this is higher or lower makes a big difference in the amount for which you could sell that bond.

Current Yield

The current yield is the interest (expressed as a percentage) based on the amount you paid for the bond (rather than on its face value). A $2,000 bond bought at par value (at $2,000) receiving 6 percent interest would earn a current yield of 6 percent. The current yield will differ if you buy the bond at a price that is higher or lower than par. For example, if you purchased a $2,000 bond with a rate of 6 percent for $1,800, you have paid less than par and bought the bond at a discount. Your yield would be higher than the straight interest rate: 6.67 percent instead of the stated 6 percent. To calculate that yield, multiply the $2,000 face value by .06 (the stated interest rate), and you get $120 (the annual interest payment). Now divide that by $1,800 (the amount you paid for the bond) to get .0667 or 6.67 percent current yield.

Average Return on Bonds

Historically, the average return on bonds, particularly on Treasury bonds, is very low compared to the return on stocks. But this is not always the case. According to a journal entitled "The Death of the Risk Premium: Consequences of the 1990s," by Arnott and Ryan (*Journal of Portfolio Management*, Spring 2001), stocks could underperform bonds in the decades ahead by about 0.9 percent a year.

Yield to Maturity

Generally considered the more meaningful number, yield to

maturity is the total amount earned on the bond from the time you buy it until it reaches maturity (assuming that you hold it to maturity). This includes interest over the life of the bond, plus any gain or loss you may incur based on whether you purchased the bond above or below par, excluding taxes. Taking the term of the bond, the cost at which you purchased it, and the yield into account, your broker will be able to calculate the yield to maturity. (You need a computer to do this; the math is extremely complicated.) Usually, this calculation factors in the coupons or interest payments being reinvested at the same rate.

Knowing the yield to maturity makes it easier to compare various bonds. Unlike stocks, which are simply bought at a specific price per share, various factors will come into play when purchasing a bond, including term of maturity, rate of interest, the price you paid for the bond, and so on. The idea here is to determine how well the bond will perform for you.

Importance of Interest Rates to Yield

Interest rates vary based on a number of factors, including the inflation rate, exchange rates, economic conditions, supply and demand of credit, actions of the Federal Reserve, and the activity of the bond market itself. As interest rates move up and down, bond prices adjust in the opposite direction; this causes the yield to fall in line with the new prevailing interest rate. By affecting bond yields via trading, the bond market thus impacts the current market interest rate.

The simplest rule of thumb to remember when dealing in the bond market is that bond prices will react opposite to interest rates. Lower interest rates mean higher bond prices, and higher interest rates mean lower bond prices. Here's why: Your bond paying 8 percent is in demand when interest rates drop, and other bonds are paying 6 percent. However, when interest rates rise, and new bonds are paying 10 percent, suddenly your 8 percent bond will be less valuable and harder to sell.

The Yield Curve

The relationship between short-term and long-term interest rates is depicted by the yield curve, a graph that illustrates the connection between bond yields and time to maturity. The yield curve allows you to compare prices among bonds with differing features (different coupon rates, different maturities, even different credit ratings). Most of the time, the yield curve looks normal (or "steep"), meaning it curves upward—short-term bonds have lower interest rates, and the rate climbs steadily as the time to maturity lengthens. Occasionally, though, the yield curve is flat or inverted. A flat yield curve, where rates are similar across the board, typically signals an impending slowdown in the economy. Short-term rates increase as long-term rates fall, equalizing the two. When short-term rates are higher than long-term rates (which can signal a recession on the horizon), you get an inverted yield curve, the opposite of the normal curve.

How Are Bonds Priced?

If you want to sell a bond or buy one on the bond market, you first need to know the latest bond prices. For this information, you can go online to a financial newspaper such as The *Wall Street Journal* or *Barron's*, or to the financial section of *USA Today* or your local paper. Bond prices do fluctuate, so the price you see quoted may change several times throughout the next business day.

Since there are far too many bonds to list—1.5 million in just the municipal bond market alone—there is no single complete listing. A single listing would not be practical, as many bondholders hang onto their bonds until maturity. Therefore, the listings you will see are benchmarks from which you can determine a fair price. Interest rates impact bond prices in a broad sense. Fixed-income securities, as a rule, will therefore be affected similarly.

In the bond listings, you will find key information for Treasury, municipal, corporate, and mortgage-backed bonds. The numbers you will see listed may vary in format from paper to paper but will include the following:

- **Rate 6.5 percent:** This is the yield that the bond is
- paying. **Maturity March 2018:** This is the date of final maturity—in this case, March of 2018.

- **Bid 103:12:** This means a buyer is offering a bid of $1,033.75 on a $1,000 bond, or a profit of just over 3 percent to the bondholder who bought the bond at a par value of $1,000. The numbers before the colon represent the percent of a par value of the bond (in this case, 103 percent of $1,000 is $1,030). The numbers after the colon are measured in 32nds of $10 (here, $^{12}/_{32}$ gives you $3.75 to add to that $1,030). This math works the same way for both the bid and ask.

- **Ask 104:00:** This is the seller's lowest asking price, in this case, $1,040.00.

You might also see an Ask/Yield entry, which gives the bond's yield to maturity based on the asking price. This shows how much the buyer will earn on the investment based on the interest rate and the cost of the bond. A buyer who bought the bond at more than the face value will receive a lower yield-to-maturity value. The opposite is true if the bond was purchased at a discount, which means it was purchased for less than par.

Stocks or Bonds?

While the stock market sees consistent gains for long-term players, its volatility can be too much for some investors. During particularly volatile periods, more investors look to the bond market. Also, as more people reinvest money from plans like 401(k)s and pension plans, bonds become attractive places to invest. They offer income as well as greater security than equities.

Bond trading is brisk, so the price you see in the paper is likely to change by the time you make your decision to buy or sell. The price will also be affected by which a broker can get you the best price on a particular bond. Don't forget that the dealers set their prices to spread their profit on the transaction.

How to Buy and Sell Bonds

Bonds are almost always purchased through brokers and brokerage houses. All the major brokerage houses handle bonds and can get you the best bond rates. They trade bonds that are already on the market and will inform you about new issues. This is true for corporate and municipal bonds as well as certain types of government bonds, such as Treasury bonds. Using a bond broker is a big commitment, though, as most demand a minimum $5,000 investment to get you started in the bond market.

If you're more of a do-it-yourself investor, you can buy Treasury bonds directly from the U.S. Treasury Department through the aptly named Treasury Direct service (*www.treasurydirect.gov*). Savings bonds can also be purchased from Treasury Direct and also through most banking institutions. Savings bonds are inexpensive—you can invest as little as $25. You won't pay any state or local income taxes on the interest, and you can buy them without paying commissions.

MUNICIPAL BONDS

Lending Money to the Government

Diversification is as important to your investment portfolio as the money that you invest in it. Stocks and mutual funds provide investors with a wide variety of options to choose from, and the bond market is no different. Bonds offer yet another means to bring diversity into your investment life. You have to understand the different types of bonds and their inherent risks and benefits.

Overview of Bond Categories

There are various types of bonds, ranging from government issued to the more speculative and even foreign company and government bonds. They have different risk and investment characteristics that can create different tax situations and may be used in a variety of ways to hedge stock exposure in a portfolio or to create an income stream for an investor. That's why it's so important to understand the critical role that bonds can play in helping you create wealth.

Five Bonds

There are five basic types of bonds for investors to choose among:

1. U.S. government securities

2. Mortgage-backed securities

3. Municipal bonds

4. Corporate bonds

5. Junk bonds (a.k.a. high-yield bonds)

Each type has its own benefits and drawbacks, and some will fit into your portfolio better than others.

Investors use bonds for two main purposes: to receive the steady income of periodic interest payments or to protect and build up their capital stores. Bonds are predictable: you know when you're going to get your principal back, and you know when to expect your next interest check. For investors looking for reliable, current income, the best choice may be bonds that have fixed interest rates until maturity and that pay interest semiannually.

On the other hand, investors saving for the future may fare better by investing in zero-coupon bonds. You won't get regular interest payments with these bonds. Instead, you buy these bonds for a deep discount, a price that's much lower than their par value. Upon maturity, you'll receive one lump payment, representing the purchase price plus earned interest, compounded semiannually at the original interest rate; basically, it's the face value, and the years of accumulated interest all rolled into one big payment.

The types of bonds you select to help you balance your portfolio should be based on your long-term investment goals. As you read on, you'll be better able to figure out which are the right bonds for your needs.

U.S. Treasury Securities

If the thought of watching a stock tumble in value makes you queasy, or if you have the need to invest in safe cash equivalents, consider U.S. Treasury bonds. Uncle Sam's gift to U.S. investors, the Treasury market offers a safe haven to battered stock investors looking for short- or long-term relief. Treasuries, as these bonds are known, are predictable and lower-yielding on average than stocks, but they are also far more secure. Generally, federal taxes must be paid on the interest, but the interest is free from state and local taxes. Treasuries are also backed by the full faith and credit of the U.S. government.

What makes Treasuries so desirable, though, is that they are highly liquid investments and can be sold quickly for cash. These securities are also easier to sell than other bonds because the government bond market is enormous. In fact, the Treasury market is the biggest securities market in the world, with an average trading volume greater than $250 billion every day. Treasuries also make good hedges against interest-rate fluctuations: Investors who buy them lock in a fixed, annual rate of return that holds firm even if rates change during the life of the bond. Treasuries come in three basic flavors:

1. **Treasury bills** (T-bills) are very short-term securities, with maturities ranging from four weeks to one year. T-bills come in $100 increments with a minimum $100 purchase and are sold at a discount from face value; the discount represents the interest income on the security.

2. **Treasury notes** come with intermediate-term maturities of two, five, and ten years. These notes are sold in $100 increments with a minimum $100 investment. They come with fixed interest rates and pay interest semiannually.

3. **Treasury bonds** are strictly long-term securities, with maturities of thirty years. They can be purchased for as little as $100. These bonds come with fixed coupon rates and pay interest every six months until maturity.

Municipal Bonds

Munis, as they're called, are very popular for their tax-free advantages. States, cities, towns, municipalities, and government entities issue them to build schools, parks, and numerous other important aspects of our communities. In exchange for your willingness to lend money to help with such worthy ventures, you not only receive interest on your loan, but your bond is usually exempt from federal—and often state—taxes. That last part is what catches people's attention since most other investments have Uncle Sam camped on your doorstep waiting to take a bite.

Not Too Bad

The yields on municipal bonds generally won't pay as much as those on their corporate counterparts. However, when you consider the yield after taxes are paid from corporate bond earnings, the munis often don't look too bad, particularly in states with high taxes. You do need to report the tax-exempt interest on tax returns for record-keeping purposes.

Not unlike corporate bonds, many municipal bonds are also rated, and those with the highest ratings rival only the government bonds in their low degree of risk. Companies such as Standard & Poor's, Moody's, and other investment services grade the bonds in the same way they grade corporate bonds. AAA (S&P) or Aaa (Moody's) are the top grades. Look for bonds with a grade of at least BBB or Bbb. As with corporate bonds, the lower the grade, the higher the risk. To ensure safety, you can get your investment secured, or in this case insured, so that you cannot lose your principal and interest due.

Municipal bonds cost $5,000 or a multiple of $5,000. Yields vary, like other bonds, based on the interest rates. Actual prices for traded bonds will be listed on the financial pages. Prices will change based on the size of the order of bonds traded and the market. Like other bonds, you can sell a muni on the secondary market and, depending on the current rate, receive a higher price than what you paid for the bond. However, if you sell a municipal bond and show a capital gain, the taxman will cometh.

If you are interested in munis, you should get to know the options available to you. Municipal bonds come in a few different types, including the following:

- **Revenue bonds.** These bonds are usually issued to fund a specific project, such as a bridge, an airport, or a highway. The revenue collected from tolls, charges, or in some manner from the project will be used to pay interest to bondholders.

- **Moral obligation bonds.** These are essentially revenue bonds offered by a state but with a unique twist. These bonds are typically issued when a state may not be able to meet the bond obligation through its normal revenue stream, which includes taxes and licenses. Just in case, the state forms a special reserve fund that can be used to pay the bond obligation, but there's no legal obligation for them to use that reserve fund, just a moral obligation. In most cases, this moral obligation—on which a state has staked its good reputation—can be even more powerful than a legal one.

- **General obligation bonds.** The issuer backs up the interest payments on these bonds by taxation. Known as GOs, these bonds are voter-approved, and the principal is backed by the full faith and credit of the issuer.

- **Taxable municipal bonds.** Why would anyone want a taxable muni if nontaxable exist? Simple: They have a higher yield, more comparable to corporate bonds, generally without much risk. Such bonds can be issued to help fund an underfunded pension plan for a municipality or to help build a ballpark for the local baseball or football team.

- **Private activity bonds.** If a bond is used for both public and private activities, it is called a private activity bond.

- **Put bonds.** These bonds allow you to redeem the bond at par value on a specific date (or dates) prior to its stated maturity. Put bonds typically come with lower-than-average yields in exchange for this flexibility, but they can make a good strategic purchase for active bond traders who expect a jump in interest rates. When rates rise sufficiently, they can cash in the put bonds (usually at par value) and reinvest in higher-yielding instruments.

- **Floating and variable-rate municipal bonds.** If it appears that the rate of interest will rise, then these are good investments because they will—as the name implies—vary the interest rates accordingly. Naturally, there's a greater interest risk involved with such bonds.

You can usually find prices of municipal bonds being traded in the financial section of a major paper or in a financial publication. Municipal brokers can then give you their own price quotes. The current market price will vary often, so if you want to buy (or sell), you need to stay on top of the current market price.

Zero-Coupon Bonds

Zero-coupon bonds can be issued by companies, government agencies, or municipalities. Known as zeros, these bonds do not pay interest periodically as most bonds do. Instead, they are purchased at a discount and pay a higher rate (both interest and principal) when they reach maturity.

No Zeros for Liquidity

Don't buy zeros (or zero-coupon bonds) for liquidity in your portfolio. As for taxes, even though you do not receive any interest payments, you need to report the amount the bond increases each year.

The interest rate is locked in when you buy the zero-coupon bond at a discount rate. For example, if you wanted to buy a five-year $10,000 zero in a municipal bond, it might cost you $7,500, and in five years, you would get the full $10,000. The longer the bond has until it reaches maturity, the deeper the discount will be. Zeros are the best example of compound interest. For example, a twenty-year zero-coupon bond with a face value of $20,000 could be purchased at a discount, for around $7,000. Since the bond is not paying out annual or semiannual dividends, the interest continues to compound, and your initial investment will earn the other $13,000. The interest rate will determine how much you will need to pay to purchase such a bond, but the compounding is what makes the discount so deep.

CORPORATE BONDS

Lending Money to a Company

When you buy shares of stock, you own a piece of a company; when you buy corporate bonds (or corporates, as they're also known), you are lending the company money for a specified amount of time and at a specific rate of interest. While corporate bonds are riskier than government or municipal bonds, long-term corporate bonds have outperformed their government and municipal counterparts over the past fifty years.

Unlike the U.S. government, however, companies can—and do—go bankrupt, which can turn your bond certificates into wallpaper. Kmart, Blockbuster, and Enron are all examples of large companies that have declared bankruptcy. Therefore, the risk of default comes into play with corporate bonds.

Corporates are generally issued in multiples of either $1,000 or $5,000. While your money is put to use for anything from new office facilities to new technology and equipment, you are paid interest annually or semiannually. Corporate bonds pay higher yields at maturity than various other bonds—though the income you receive is taxable at both the federal and state level.

If you plan to hold onto the bond until it reaches maturity and you are receiving a good rate of return for doing so, you should not worry about selling in the secondary market. The only ways in which you will not see your principal returned upon maturity is if the bond is called, has a sinking-fund provision, or the company defaults.

Bond Calls

A call will redeem the bonds before their stated maturity. This usually occurs when the issuer wants to issue a new bond series at a lower interest rate. A bond that can be called will have what is known as a call provision, stating exactly when the issuer can call in their bond if they so choose. A fifteen-year bond might stipulate that it can be called after eight years. Reinvesting in a bond that has been called will usually involve lower rates. Since the call will change the mathematics, your yield to maturity won't be the same.

Sinking-Fund Provision

A sinking-fund provision means that earnings within the company are being used to retire a certain number of bonds annually. The bond provisions will indicate clearly that they have such a feature. Each year enough cash is available, a portion of the bonds will be retired, which are usually chosen by lottery. Whether the bonds you're holding are selected is merely the luck of the draw. Unlike a call provision, you may not see anything above the face value when the issuer retires the bond. On the other hand, since the company uses the money to repay debts, these bonds likely won't default, making them a lower-risk investment.

There are a few other reasons why bonds can be called early, and those are written into the bond provisions when you purchase them. As is the case, when you buy any investment, you need to read everything carefully when buying bonds. There are numerous possibilities when it comes to bonds and bond provisions. Again, read all bond provisions very carefully before purchasing.

High-Yield Bonds

Known in the financial world by their official name, high-yield bonds, but known to many investors as junk bonds, these bonds can provide a higher rate of return or higher yield than most other bonds. Junk bonds are risky investments, as investors saw in the 1980s debacle involving Ivan Boesky and Michael Milken. These two infamous financiers brought an awareness of junk bonds to the mainstream when their use of this risky debt to finance other endeavors came crashing down. The "junk bond kings" issued debt with nothing backing it up. When it came time to pay up, the money just wasn't there, and investors were left holding worthless pieces of paper—hence the term junk bonds.

High-yield bonds are bonds that didn't make the grade. They are issued by companies that are growing, reorganizing, or are considered at greater risk of defaulting on the bond, for whatever reason. These bonds are often issued when companies are merging and have debts to pay in such a transaction. They are used as a method of financing such acquisitions.

High-yield or junk bonds include risk of default and risk that their market value will drop quickly. Since the companies that issue these bonds are not as secure as those issuing high-grade bonds, their stock prices may drop, bringing the market value of the bond down with it. This will mean that trading such a bond will become very difficult, therefore eliminating their liquidity.

Fallen Angels

Before the 1980s, most junk bonds resulted when investment-grade issuers experienced a decline in credit quality, brought on by big changes in business conditions or when they took on too much financial risk. These issuers were known as fallen angels.

Sometimes a company begins by issuing lower-grade high-yield bonds and does well, with their sales numbers going up. Eventually, this company reaches a level at which they can issue higher-grade bonds. This means that in the short term, you can receive high yields from their original low-grade bonds. It also means that they will call the bonds as soon as they can issue bonds at a lower yield.

If you see a company with great potential that has not yet hit its stride, perhaps you will want to take a shot at a high-yield bond from that company. If you are not that daring, you might opt for a high yield bond mutual fund, which diversifies your investment so that you are not tossing all your eggs into one high-risk basket. In this manner, if one company defaults, you are still invested in others in the fund, some of which may prosper.

Mortgage-Backed Securities

A popular bond category since the 1980s, mortgage-backed

securities (MBS) can be a highly profitable, extremely complicated, and highly risky investment option. The keyword here, though, is complicated, and the intricacies of some of these securities (particularly the CMO, or collateralized mortgage obligation, variety) make them inappropriate for novice investors. In fact, they were largely implicated in the big financial meltdown of 2008. But the most basic form of these bonds, the MBS, can make a good addition to an income-focused portfolio.

Financial institutions help create mortgage-backed securities by selling part of their residential mortgage portfolios to investors. Investors basically buy a piece of a pool of mortgages. An investor in mortgage-backed security sees profit from the cash flow (people's mortgage payments) generated from the pool of residential mortgages. As mortgage payments come in, interest and principal payments are made to the investors.

There are several types of mortgage-related securities available today. One of the most common is the pass-through Ginnie Mae, issued by the Government National Mortgage Association (GNMA), an agency of the federal government. The GNMA guarantees that investors will receive timely interest and principal payments. Investors receive potentially high-interest payments, consisting of both principal and interest. The rate of principal repayment varies with current interest rates.

Choosing Bonds for Your Portfolio

One of the keys to successful bond investing is diversification.

Holding a range of maturities—a strategy commonly called laddering —helps ensure your portfolio won't take too big a hit when interest rates go wild. Your bond ladder should have an average maturity that meshes with your overall financial plan— and that helps diversify your portfolio as a whole. In addition, holding bonds with different risk characteristics can increase your returns with a margin of safety.

As you're deciding which bonds to buy, there are several more personal issues you'll need to consider. Taxes are first on the list. Some bonds, mainly government bonds, offer some tax advantages that may be very attractive to someone in a higher tax bracket. At the same time, though, holding tax-exempt bonds could cause the alternative minimum tax rules to kick in, increasing your tax bill. Another factor to consider is your inflation situation: If the rest of your income is relatively safe from the negative effects of inflation, you may not have to make risky bond choices to stay ahead.

Generally speaking, most people do best when the bulk of their bond investments are high quality, meaning treasuries, munis, and high-grade corporate bonds. Mixing these three types together is better than focusing on only one. These types of debt securities balance out the risk of the stock portion of your portfolio in a way that junk bonds cannot. And investors looking for big returns may be better off allocating a little more to the stock market than investing in high-risk, high-yield bonds.

Chapter 6: Investing in real estate

The details of real estate investment can be overwhelming. There's a whole new language to learn: closing costs, resale value, liquidity, and inspections. But if you're willing to overcome your apprehensions, you'll find that real estate can be a wise investment. If you are considering investing in real estate, it's important that you do your research so that your investment will turn into a profitable venture. It's harder to get out of real estate than a stock or bond purchase, so educate yourself and make sure you understand exactly what you're doing.

A real estate investment is generally tangible—you buy land or property that you can actually see. Think about how stocks and bonds work. You invest your money in a company you do not physically own. By buying shares, you are, in essence, lending the company your money and hoping for a profit. With real estate, you own the "company," so you need to sell "shares" of it to see a profit— by selling or renting the property.

LEVERAGING

The Power of Debt

Leverage, plain and simple, is debt; it's using other people's money to buy what you want, which actually allows you to use less of your own money to get more property. In real estate investing, leverage can make or break your portfolio. With the right amount of debt taken out on the right lucrative properties, you can make a killing in real estate using very little of your own money. But there's a downside: too much debt or unaffordable debt coupled with shrinking property values can spell financial disaster. There's a pretty fine line between the two, and as long as you stand firmly on the profitable side, real estate investing can provide solid returns— but it will take a lot of legwork on your part to pull this off.

Inflation

You must consider inflation when investing in real estate. Believe it or not, a real estate investor can reap profits from inflation alone. Check out this example. An investor has $30,000 worth of equity in a $100,000 property. With a 3 percent inflationary increase in property values, her holdings are now worth $103,000 —a $3,000 increase. That $3,000 increase on her $30,000 investment translates into a 10 percent return —due solely to inflation.

Here's the key to success: You have to be smart about your borrowing. Never borrow more than you can afford to pay back. Always understand all the terms of your loan contract, particularly if you take on an adjustable interest rate (also called a variable interest rate). Don't let anyone talk you into a loan that doesn't make sense.

Bubbles and Scams

A big part of the Great Recession of 2008–09 was an

overinflated real estate market. Urged on by brokers, many people purchased homes beyond what they could afford. Particularly dangerous were adjustable-rate mortgages, in which the mortgage premium suddenly— often dramatically— increased after several years. Many of these homes went into foreclosure.

Be alert as well for scams. If someone tells you that you can buy a property with "no money down," ask yourself if this offer sounds too good to be true. If it does, it probably is.

When you borrow wisely, you can use the bank's money to acquire and improve investment properties. At the same time, you can invest your own money in other ways. This means more money is going to work for you, which increases your portfolio's profit potential. When everything goes your way—you quickly flip a property for a profit or immediately land a golden tenant who always pays the rent on time— you can pay back the loan with your investment cash flow and keep a tidy profit for yourself.

Of course, there's a downside. When circumstances are less favorable, as they usually are, you may end up struggling to pay the investment property loan. That's why it's critically important only to get a loan you can afford to pay back even if you don't get a tenant or can't sell the property right away.

FLIPPING HOUSES

Speculation in Real Estate

Real estate is a risky business, and there are no guarantees on every piece of land or property. Be careful and educate yourself before dropping a big chunk of change on any property. First, you need to know the difference between speculators and investors.

Real estate speculators aren't the same as investors. Speculators buy and sell quickly in order to make a fast profit. Investors seek out long-term gains and look for what they can afford to keep for the long haul. You must consider your finances carefully to determine which option is right for you. If real estate investing is new to you, hold off on speculation until you're more familiar with the market. And consider consulting a property specialist to help you get your feet wet without getting soaked.

For the novice real estate investor who wants to own physical property, there are two good options: small rental properties (like single- or two-family homes or four-apartment buildings) or a house that requires some fixing up. Of all the ways you can invest in real estate, single-family houses may offer the clearest opportunities for new investors, mainly because they're very easy to acquire and usually easy to sell.

Hiring Professionals

If you take a day to paint instead of hiring a painter, do you really save that much? If you hire a painter, you can spend the day finding another bargain property— perhaps one with a $20,000 profit margin. If it takes you 100 hours to find, fix, and sell this property, you have, in essence, paid yourself $200 an hour!

You may be able to reap big profits by buying older, run-down homes and restoring them for resale. This is a very common way for investors to approach real estate, and while it can bring in some tidy profits for some, it's not for everyone. Here are some factors that you'll need to consider before making the decision to invest in a fixer-upper:

- **Expertise.** You'll need to know at least something about building design and construction in order to have an idea of how much work (and money) it will take to get the house into good shape. Figure out what you can do yourself and also how much it will cost you to hire someone else to do it. Remember to factor costs for building materials, contractors, and your time into the property's purchase price.

- **Staying power.** Do you have the patience to withstand the problems that are bound to crop up as you restore the property? Real estate can be a bigger commitment than many people expect. Plus, in down markets, property— even fixed up, premium property—can be difficult to sell for a profit, and you may have to wait for prices to go up again.

- **Inspection.** Hire a professional home inspector to do a comprehensive inspection of any property before you agree to purchase it. It's critical to be fully informed of all the potential pitfalls you might encounter once you start rehabbing the property, but keep in mind that no inspector will be able to spot all the problems.

- **Location.** The location of the property is the most important factor to consider. Study the neighborhood, shopping, and transportation facilities. Think about how the property can be used based on its location and zoning. Residential rental property in a good school district will attract young families. Property with easy highway access could be very valuable for commercial purposes.

Location Tip

Seasoned house flippers suggest that one way to look at the location is this: Buy the worst house in the best neighborhood. Through your hard work, you can improve the house and sell it for a profit. Bringing back a neighborhood is a much longer, more expensive process and involves many more people.

If you want to invest in commercial property or executive rentals, look for property within thirty miles of a city. If you are willing to look outside the cities, you can usually find inexpensive land. If you discover a tract of land that appeals to you but is not listed for sale, you might be able to track down the owner by visiting the county register or calling the county appraiser's office. You can always contact the owner with an offer—she just might be willing to sell.

Get Rental Insurance

If you decide to rent your investment property, be prepared to get rental insurance and property insurance. Your homeowner's policy most likely won't cover renters, and you need protection against any damage done by your tenants. This also covers you if tenants try to blame injuries on you.

Real estate professionals will suggest you to stay conventional in your real estate investment strategies and not to buy white elephants. Of course, you must also look for hidden defects in the property before you buy. If you find any problems after the purchase, you will be the one who has to fix them, especially if you're trying to make the property attractive for resale. Pay attention to what's going on locally, and be sure your planned purchase makes sense. Will there be a demand for this kind of property in five or ten years? Always be on the lookout for things that make a sale easier, like a bargain property or extraordinary features.

Potentially profitable real estate opportunities exist during good economic times and bad, but it is critical to make wise decisions and pick carefully to get the best deals. This can be a tricky proposition for any investor, especially when property values are at their peak or when a tight credit market makes securing a loan seem harder than winning the lottery. The following example illustrates why you should take demand and location into account in purchasing a property. After watching their children grow up and go off to college, a couple decided they did not need such a big house any longer, so they bought a beautiful place in upstate New York that needed some work. They made improvements and additions, and after just two years, the house had increased in its appraised value. However, the house next door was empty. The bank had foreclosed on it, and the structure sat empty and unkempt. Furthermore, an important local industry was laying off workers. To make a long story short, the couple saw that if they wanted to sell, they would have to drop their asking price substantially.

A house with an empty property next door in an economically depressed area is not desirable enough to sell for its appraised value.

Any property is only worth what the buyer is willing to pay for it.

RENTAL PROPERTIES

Long-Term Investments

If you are considering making a real estate purchase for rental purposes, you will choose between commercial and residential property. You need to assess your own financial situation first, as this is not the most liquid investment. It's important to determine how much money you will need upfront, how much money you can borrow, and what the terms of the loan will be. Investment capital is the first item on your agenda. If you do not have it, you'll need to borrow it. New investors are usually advised not to borrow for the purpose of buying real estate. Unlike stocks or bonds, you cannot start out with a $100 investment.

Tax Benefits

Real estate investing can come with a big tax benefit. Special tax incentives for real estate investors can make a big difference in your ultimate tax liability. Rental property deductions may be used to offset other income. In fact, tax breaks can transform real estate losses into profits.

Make sure you do all your homework about a property's location, even if you think it's a once-in-a-lifetime deal. A house that seems like a steal today may not seem like such a great deal in a few months when a major highway construction project comes through its front lawn. Find out from the local municipality what building projects are slated nearby— particularly projects like schools, highways, shopping centers, and industrial or commercial centers. All of these developments can impact traffic issues and property values. Sometimes a great property offered at a great price means the seller knows something you don't know about an upcoming event that will impact the resale value of the property. If you are purchasing a commercial or residential property with the idea of renting it out or selling it in the future, you need to consider the following:

- Is this a prime location? Remember, location still means everything in real estate.

- Has this property been rented successfully before?

- How old is the property?

- Has it been thoroughly inspected and given a clean bill of health? You may need to arrange for this yourself, thoroughly inspecting and fixing electricity, plumbing, and the foundation and roof. Everything must comply with local safety ordinances.

- How much renovation and work need to be put into this property? This will follow, in part, from the inspections. Changing the interior to fit your business or rental needs is a significant cost factor.

- How much will it cost to maintain the property? Do you need gardeners? Will a janitor be needed on the premises at all times?

  Upkeep is important in evaluating the potential resale or rental value of the property.

- What are the zoning laws in the area? This is particularly important if you are opening a new type of business in a commercial property.

- What is the accessibility to and from the property? You may find the perfect little hideaway for a summer rental, but a business property will need to be accessible.

- What plans are being carried out for the future of the area? Is a new highway coming through that would help your business by providing high visibility, or will it ruin the vacation value of your secluded villa?

- How much insurance will you need? What are the rates for that property in conjunction with the purposes of your investment?

- What property taxes are applicable? What can be deducted?

If this list hasn't scared you off, you might be the ideal real estate investor. Not unlike investing in stocks, there is an issue of timing when it comes to investing in real estate. The stock market, over time, tends to end up ahead. Real estate should work as well. However, the economic climate can change, so real estate, like any other investment, can be risky.

Managing Your Rental Properties

In addition to the money, there are other complex aspects of buying real estate to rent or sell. It's important that you have good management skills and an eye for detail, as there are numerous details involved with any property. You need to be able to maintain the property, which means proper upkeep. You have to factor that into your costs. Unless you are very handy, you will need to know how and where to find the right electricians, plumbers, and contractors. Maintaining a property is a major responsibility; unlike stocks or bonds, you are responsible for keeping this investment in good condition.

If you decide to make the leap and purchase a rental property, you will be entering the world of the landlord. If you have been a renter, you know a good landlord can make life easy, while a bad landlord can make life miserable. How you act as a landlord will have a great impact on the well-being of your investment.

Check Renter History

Always check a renter's credit history, background, and references. Suppose you don't screen your tenants and select them carefully. In that case you could encounter numerous problems later: a tenant who's always late with the rent, damages your property, moves in objectionable friends, or worse.

Problems will arise in any rental situation, and the way you handle them is important to maintaining the property at a reasonable cost. It's far easier to make an effort to maintain a property when it's your own residence. However, you'll have to do as much work—if not more—to protect your investment. If the investment is taking up too much of your time, you are basically losing income. That's time you could be spending earning money somewhere else. If you are spending hours maintaining a property, you are cutting into your income-earning time and losing money in the process. People choose stocks, bonds, and mutual funds as investments partly because they require little work to maintain.

Good communication with your tenants is crucial to your ability to be a good landlord and to protect your valuable investment. Tenants need to understand your expectations, as well as your rules and regulations, in advance of entering into an agreement to lease your property. Any changes in the rules need to be expressed and explained in writing with sufficient notice to tenants. Make sure all communications with tenants are done in writing and that you can prove the communication was delivered to the tenant.

No matter what shape it's in, you cannot expect to buy a rental property, immediately find tenants, and then just walk away and let the monthly rental checks roll in. If you aren't prepared to manage your rental property, or if you just don't have the time, hire a professional property manager. Property managers take care of daily repair and upkeep issues, landscaping needs, tenant concerns and complaints, and collecting rent. Fees vary based on the level of work required and the size of the building involved. You can hire an individual to do this work or contract with a management company. If you think you're going to need a professional manager to handle your rental property, make sure you factor that cost into your decision to buy the property and the rental costs you pass on to your tenants.

TRUSTS

Another Real Estate Option

If you're not ready to jump into a real estate investment as an owner or landlord, there is another option that allows you to reap the benefits of real estate investing without all of the negatives of property ownership. A real estate investment trust (or REIT, pronounced "reet") offers investors a way to invest in commercial real estate in much the same way they would invest in the stock market. In short, a REIT lets you invest in real estate without having to actually buy property or land. There are more than 200 REITs to choose from, and shares of REITs are traded much like shares of stock. In fact, you can find REITs listed on the stock exchanges.

Less popular than stocks, funds, and even bonds, REITs are not new. They were established more than fifty years ago as a safe way to get into the real estate market. They are more liquid, and therefore more attractive than direct investments in real estate; selling shares of a REIT is as easy as selling a mutual fund or stock. Since you don't actually own the real estate, you don't suffer the hassles that come with property ownership. On the other hand, a REIT gives you none of the rights that come with property ownership, either.

REITs share the characteristics of both stocks and mutual funds. A REIT is a publicly-traded company, so owning shares is similar to owning shares of stocks. On the other hand, REITs were created to follow the paradigm of investment companies or mutual funds. Since most small investors cannot invest directly in income-producing real estate, a REIT allows them to pool their investment resources and is, therefore, like a mutual fund. This investment type is called pass-through security, passing through the income from the property to the shareholders. The income is not taxed at the corporate level but at the investor level.

What's in the REIT?

Unlike mutual funds, which purchase stock in companies, REITs focus on all types of real estate investments. These investments usually take one of two forms. An equity REIT buys actual property (with the property's equity representing the investment). A mortgage REIT invests in mortgages that provide financing for the purchase of properties. In the latter, the income comes from the interest on those mortgages. Of course, like everything else, there's always one option that fits in the gray area in between. In this case, that's known as a hybrid REIT, which does a little of each.

When comparing REITs and deciding which is best for you, you need to consider several factors. Here are some important areas to look at when you start comparing different REITs:

1. **Dividend yield.** Review how much the REIT offers when paying dividends and how that compares to the price of the stock. The dividend yield is the dividend paid per share, divided by the price of the stock. So if the price goes down, the dividend yield goes up. Dividends in 2014 averaged 6.9 percent for REITs—compared with 1.9 percent for S&P 500 companies.

2. **Earnings growth.** With REITs, the magic earnings number is called funds from operations, or FFO. The FFO indicates the true performance of the REIT, which can't really be seen with the same kind of net income calculation used by standard corporations. A REIT's FFO equals its regular net income (for accounting purposes), excluding gains or losses from property sales and debt restructuring and adding back real estate depreciation.

3. **Types of investments held.** Identify what properties the REIT invests in. REITs can invest in office buildings, shopping malls, and retail locations; residential property, including apartment complexes, hotels, and resorts; healthcare facilities; and various other forms of real estate.

4. **Geographic locations.** Check out where the REIT invests. Some REITs invest on a national level, and others specialize in regions of the country.

5. **Diversification.** There's that word again. Whether you choose a REIT that diversifies across state borders or buy several REITs with the idea of investing in everything from small motels to massive office complexes, you should always favor diversification when investing, and that includes investing in REITs.

6. **Management.** Much like buying shares in a mutual fund, you are purchasing an investment run by professional management. You should look at the background of the manager. In this case, you'll be looking for someone with a real estate background. REIT managers often have extensive experience that may have begun in a private company that later went public as the person continued on with the company.

Just as you investigate a company issuing shares of stock, you have to investigate the company behind your REIT. You must also look at the real estate market and the economic conditions in the area or areas where your REIT is doing business.

REITs Compared with the S&P 500

Over the thirty-year span ending December 31, 2013, the compound annual total return for equity REITs was approximately 11.7 percent. Compare that with the S&P 500 return during the same stretch of time, which came in lower at 10.8 percent (data from *www.nareit.com*).

Tracking Your REITs

You'll see share prices for your REIT quoted daily, so you can follow your investment pretty much the same way you would track a mutual fund. The best measure of your REIT's performance is its FFO, which is often referred to simply as earnings. The FFO differs from corporate earnings, mainly in the area of depreciation. For corporations that have assets like computers and tractors, all physical assets (except land) depreciate, meaning they record a decline in value. That makes sense because they really do lose value over time. However, real estate typically maintains or increases its value. A company whose main holding is real estate calculates its earnings, or FFO, by starting with the standard net income number, adding back depreciation on real estate and other non-cash items, and removing the effect of some capital transactions. This way, you can see a clearer picture of what kind of cash the REIT is really generating.

All in all, if you are a beginning investor who believes the time is right to invest in real estate, the best choice is a REIT. This form of investment provides a cost-effective way to invest in income-producing properties that you otherwise would not have the opportunity (or the capital) to become involved in. Regardless of how you get into real estate, whether through a REIT or as a property owner, it can be a lucrative and worthwhile investment strategy.

Chapter 7: Your investment portfolio and investor profile

Now that you've got a good idea of the kinds of investments you can make and some of the various investing strategies you can employ, it's time to create your portfolio. A lot of this will depend on what kind of a person you are: your goals, your dreams, and your personality. An investment portfolio is a very personal thing. In this chapter, you'll explore what you have to do to create a portfolio that both reflects you and will make money for you.

INVESTING GOALS

Planning Your Future

Once you've compiled a current financial snapshot and gained a good understanding of how you handle your money, it's time to take the next step along the path. Now that you know where you stand, you can figure where you want to go. It's time to set your investing goals.

First, make your goals specific and measurable. Don't say you want to save more; say you want to save $1,000 over the next twelve months. Instead of dreaming about some far-off retirement on a tropical island, set a goal to retire with $6 million when you're sixty-five. With goals like these, you can mark your progress and make adjustments as necessary to help you hit your targets.

Remember Inflation

When you set your financial goals, remember to take inflation into account. Traditionally, inflation has averaged about 3 percent annually.

The second rule is to allow for the unexpected, a critical part of every investment plan. Your car may break down, your hot water heater may stop working (probably while you're in the shower), or you might need a trip to the ER. All of these events take you by surprise, and they all cost money—money you were expecting to use in different ways, and probably at different times. To deal with unexpected expenditures, you'll need to have some easily accessible cash—but that doesn't mean uninvested cash. By planning for the unexpected and keeping some of your investment assets highly liquid, you'll be able to deal with situations like these without veering too far off your goal path. Remember, the reverse can happen, too. Whenever you get your hands on extra cash—like a pay raise, a bonus, or a loan finally paid off—use it to pay down debt or add to savings and investments.

Make sure to include your expected retirement needs. If your lifestyle tones down, some advisors figure you'll need 60–70 percent of your current income. For more intricate calculations—like the potential effects of inflation and investment returns—check in with a financial planner, or try some retirement-planning software.

Assess your current savings stage and plan your holdings accordingly. The further you are from your goal's timeline, the more risks you can afford to take with your investments. The key to all of this: *Start saving money now.*

Finally, design a preliminary investment plan that will move you toward meeting your financial goals. It can take time to refine and perfect your plan, but a basic model (such as the aging method, where you convert your age to a percentage and invest that portion of your holdings in bonds and cash and the rest in stocks) is a good place to start. At the same time, your first instinct may be to take a chunk of cash and buy a hot stock. That probably isn't the best way to get where you want to go. Impulse investing, like impulse buying, can drain your money without giving you anything in return. So start with a basic plan until you gain some more knowledge and experience, or hire a professional to help you. Then, while your money is already beginning to work for you, you can take the time to plan an appropriate portfolio specific to your goals and timeline. That is the way to build your fortune and keep it intact.

Some independent research will be necessary. This includes due diligence on companies where you're considering parking some of your investment dollars, as well as portfolio tracking and performance monitoring.

Your Investment Choices

Having all the ingredients for success is a good start, but you won't get too far without the recipe. If you take all the ingredients for a delicious pastry and throw them together in equal parts, you'll end up with an inedible brick. Developing the art of measuring and mixing your ingredients, so they work together to create investment perfection requires patience and diligence on your part.

Components of a Portfolio

Most investment portfolios consist of several components. Usually, they include some combination of the following:

- Liquid assets (cash and equivalents)

- Fixed-income securities (bonds and annuities)

- Equities (stocks)

- Real estate

- Commodities (precious metals) Other investments

Figuring out which securities will constitute your portfolio isn't a difficult process, as long as you apply the tried-and-true investment tenets: knowing your risk levels, having a fixed time horizon, employing investment diversification (through your asset allocation), and having set investment goals. Two of the more important factors in your portfolio decision-making process are risk and diversification.

Personalizing Your Investments

Managing your own expectations is a big part of your

investment planning process, and it starts with figuring out exactly what kind of investor you are. Once you know that, the rest of your investment planning will fall into place much more easily. Though there are many subtle variations in investor profiles, the two main types are buy-and-hold and market timing. Where you are along the time horizon, your risk tolerance, and your personal style all factor into the type of investor, you will be.

Here are some good questions to ask yourself to determine your investor profile:

1. Do market fluctuations keep me awake at night?

2. Am I unfamiliar with investing?

3. Do I consider myself more a saver than an investor?

4. Am I fearful of losing 25 percent of my assets in a few days or weeks?

5. Am I comfortable with the ups and downs of the securities markets?

6. Am I knowledgeable about investing and the securities markets?

7. Am I investing for a long-term goal?

8. Can I withstand considerable short-term losses?

If you answered yes to the first four questions, you are most likely a conservative investor. If you answered yes to the last four questions, you are more likely an aggressive investor. If you fall somewhere in between, you could call yourself a moderate investor. Conservative investors typically follow the buy-and-hold strategy, whereas aggressive investors are often market timers. As you might expect, moderate investors tend to mix the two types into one blended profile.

Buy-and-Hold Investing

When it comes to buy-and-hold investing, you may have heard that it doesn't really matter what the market is doing when you get in, as long as you stay in. There's a great deal of truth in that line of thinking. Studies show that stocks can grow on average up to 10 to 12 percent annually, and long-term U.S. Treasury instruments can grow at a rate of up to 6 to 8 percent per year. Combined with the miracle of compounding, a long-term outlook coupled with a solid, disciplined investment strategy can yield big bucks over twenty, thirty, and especially forty-plus years.

The trick is in staying in the markets and not missing their sharp upturns. People who engage in market timing—market timers, those Wall Street daredevils who try to get in and out of the stock market at the most optimal moments—risk missing those market spikes. And that money is hard to make back.

The Downside of Market Timing

Market timers also generally experience higher transaction costs compared to those of a buy-and-hold strategy. Every time an investor sells or buys securities, a transaction fee is incurred. Even if the market timer achieves above-average returns, the transaction costs could negate the superior performance. Plus, trying to time the market can create additional risk. Consider the time period from 1962 to 1991. An investor who bought common stocks in 1962 would have realized a return of 10.3 percent with a buy-and-hold strategy. If that same investor tried to time the market and missed just twelve of the best-performing months (out of a total of 348 months), the return would have been only 5.4 percent. It must be admitted that there's a flip side to this theory. If the investor had jumped out of the market during its worst periods (like the 1987 crash and several subsequent bear markets), returns would have been even higher than if he'd stayed invested during the downturns.

One additional negative aspect of using market-timing techniques is tax reporting complications. Going in and out of the market several times in one tax year (sometimes several times in a month) generates numerous taxable gain and loss transactions, all of which must be accounted for on your income tax return.

Chapter 8: Education and retirement planning

Two of the biggest concerns people have in life are planning the costs of their children's education and saving for retirement.

Education costs continue to spiral; as of 2015, the average cost of a four-year education at a private school was a staggering $169,676. Student debt has increased at an alarming rate. The average student of the class of 2015 will be paying off $35,000 in student loans—for certain fields such as medicine and law, the amounts are considerably higher.

Although many strategies for coping with these costs have been suggested, one that many people are considering is strategic financial investing. Wisely invested, a small monetary stake can be parlayed into an education nest egg.

This is just as true of the costs of retirement. Most potential retirees have not saved enough to cover the gap between their living expenses and the money they will receive from Social Security. When pensions are rapidly becoming a thing of the past, investing for retirement is an attractive alternative.

INVESTING FOR EDUCATION

Preparing Your Child's Future

College costs are rising at an alarming pace. In order to make sure your kids will have the benefit of higher education; you need to start saving right now. Luckily, several investment options can help you send your kids to college— without sacrificing your retirement. You can invest in state-sponsored plans, like a 529 plan, or you can set up your own plan, similar to an IRA. In fact, you can even do both. Whatever you decide, though, your best bet is to start right away.

Start Planning for College Tuition Now

If you take nothing else away from this chapter, remember this: Start saving now for your children's college tuition, or a lot of choices could fall off the table. If you don't have children yet, start saving as soon as you begin thinking about having them. By starting earlier, you have more opportunity to let the power of compounding work for you, building your savings faster. Total college costs today can run close to $14,000 a year for state schools and a whopping $41,000 and up for private schools.

Let's take a step back, though. How can you figure out how much to put away for a college education that won't begin for ten or twenty years? Quick and easy answer: online calculators. These can help you figure out the whole cost of college: tuition, books, room and board, and even living expenses. Depending on your singular situation, you may also need to figure in transportation expenses if your child goes to school far from home.

Calculate Financial Aid

Just because one college costs more than another doesn't

necessarily mean you'll pay more out of pocket to send your child there. More expensive schools often offer more financial aid. That aid can translate into a lower cost than if you sent your child to a school with lower tuition.

To use the Sallie Mae site for long-term planning, you'll be asked to fill in some basic information:

- The current cost of attending the college of choice

- The number of years left until your child will be starting college How much money you already have saved and earmarked for college costs

- The expected rate of return on your investments

Once you've come up with a projected bottom line, the site offers suggestions to help you create a savings plan to help you cope with the rising costs. Their first step is: In the form of scholarship, directing you toward all the potential sources of free money.

Tax-Sheltered Education Savings

Regular investments inevitably lead to tax bills, and that eats into your investment dollars. Until fairly recently, that was the only way to save money for college. Now, though, you have tax-advantaged choices, options that let your money grow tax-deferred, and (in some cases) let you use the money with no tax bill attached.

Ask an Accountant

The tax code offers breaks in the form of education tax credits and deductions. Ask your tax accountant if you're eligible to claim either the Hope credit or the Lifetime Learning credit. You may also be able to take advantage of special deductions for tuition and fees or student loan interest that you've paid.

Why is tax-deferred growth so important? It lets you keep more of your money working for you and lets your nest egg grow faster than it would if you had to keep depleting it to pay taxes on your earnings. This works in the same way as retirement savings. The more taxes you can avoid, the better.

There are three kinds of tax advantages you can look for. First, the money you put away now isn't taxed or becomes temporarily tax-deductible. Second, the earnings aren't taxable now. Third, the money doesn't get taxed when you withdraw it to pay for college. Not all college investments offer this triple play; some of them don't offer any tax advantages at all. As you look for the savings vehicles that work best for your family situation, remember to consider the current and future impact that taxes will have on your hard-earned money.

All about 529 Plans

Qualified tuition plans, also known as 529 plans, have changed the college savings playing ground. These state-sponsored plans serve up significant tax advantages, making it easier than ever to save for a college education. There are two major types of 529 plans: college savings plans (the type most people think of when they hear 529) and prepaid tuition plans.

Only for College

If you use the money from a college savings plan on expenses that don't qualify, you'll be subject to a hefty tax penalty on your earnings: an extra 10 percent on top of the regular taxes that will be due. For example, transportation to the school and dorm room decorating items do not qualify as education expenses.

College savings plans allow an account holder (usually a parent or grandparent) to set up an account for a future student (formally called the beneficiary). As the account holder, you make decisions about the account, which can include investment choices, though these may be limited depending on the state sponsoring the plan. When it's college time, you can use the funds in this 529 plan to pay for all "qualified higher education costs," which include fees, books, and computers along with tuition and room and board. And as long as you use the money for such qualified expenses, you won't have to pay federal income taxes; in most cases, the funds will be exempt from state income taxes, too. In fact, many states give their residents a current tax deduction for contributions to the home state 529 plan; some states even give you a deduction if you contribute to any state's plan.

Another huge advantage of these plans is the enormous contribution limit. You can get these tax-advantaged savings on contributions as large as $300,000 in some states. Plus, there are no income limitations, meaning you can't get phased out of the tax benefits on these plans. Of course, there's still a little tax catch (there always is): The contributions could be subject to federal (and possibly state) gift taxes. As of this printing date, gifts larger than $14,000 (or $28,000 from a couple or $70,000 over five years) are typically subject to gift-tax reporting. Luckily, there's a special exception that specifically addresses 529 plan contributions: A couple can put up to $100,000 into a qualified state tuition plan, and it will count as $20,000 over five years, nullifying the whole gift-tax issue. But they can't make any more gift-tax-free contributions until that five years is up.

It all sounds good, but there are some disadvantages. For example, you have limited control over where your money gets invested. Typically, the state invests the funds for you from a very limited menu. In some states, you may have as few as two investment choices, up to thirty in others. Plus, you can only change your choices once a year. Also, funds in a 529 plan account reduce the amount of financial aid available to the student.

Coverdell Education Savings Accounts

A Coverdell education savings account (ESA) is a tax-advantaged way to save for college with a unique, beneficial twist: The money can be used for any education expenses, including primary and secondary school. And while the contributions to the ESA are not tax-deductible, the earnings on the account are tax-free when you use them to pay for qualified education expenses.

Limiting Aid

An ESA can severely limit (or even completely eliminate) the amount of financial aid your child would be otherwise eligible for. That's because the account is considered to be the child's asset, which is given extra weight when financial aid calculations are made.

To get started, you open an ESA at your bank (or other financial institution, like your brokerage firm) for each child who will benefit; three children would mean three separate ESAs. While each ESA can only be opened for one child, one child can have more than one ESA opened in his name.

Every year, you can contribute up to $2,000 into ESAs for a single beneficiary; if one child has more than one ESA, the total annual contribution among them is limited to $2,000. If more is contributed for a single child (even if the money comes from different taxpayers), the consequence is a tax penalty on the excess. You can, though, make multiple $2,000 contributions if you have more than one child. Contributions can only be made until the child turns eighteen, with one exception: You can contribute any amount in the same year you use funds to pay for tuition.

As you probably expect by now, there are other hurdles to cross. Let's start with the income limitations; how much money you earn limits the amount of money you can put into the ESA. Single taxpayers earning less than $95,000 or joint taxpayers earning less than $190,000 can contribute the full amount. Earn more than that, though, and your maximum contribution drops until it's fully phased out when single earnings hit $110,000, and joint earnings hit $220,000. In addition, the funds have to be used by the time the beneficiary turns thirty.

Let's not overlook the very real advantages of the ESA, though. Unlike other college savings vehicles, you have complete control over the investments. You can invest the ESA funds in virtually anything: mutual funds, stocks, bonds, or whatever you think will work. You can open the account wherever you want. And the ability to use these for any level of education makes them very flexible: You can send your child to private kindergarten with this money if you want to. Finally, you can contribute to both an ESA and a 529 (in most cases), allowing you more control of your child's future.

Prepaid Tuition Plans

State-sponsored prepaid tuition plans fall under the 529

umbrella, but they are quite different than standard college savings plans.

Though the details vary from state to state, the basic idea is standard.

Parents pay money now to purchase future college tuition.

There are a lot of benefits here. To start, you pay today's tuition cost regardless of when your child will be attending. That payment secures you a guarantee that your child will be entitled to go to college in the future, no matter how much it costs then. Though most of these plans are designed for state schools, many states include built-in flexibility that allows the funds to be used toward out-of-state or private colleges. If you don't end up using the account to send your child to college, you can transfer the account to another relative, hold onto it for grandchildren, or even get a full or partial refund. One big downside, though: These plans reduce your child's eligibility for financial aid dollar-for-dollar. So if your child wants to go to a private school and the prepaid plan doesn't cover the whole cost, you probably won't be able to turn to financial aid.

Which Plan to Choose?

Exactly what the plan offers depends on the state sponsoring it. While all states offer full prepaid tuition for four-year colleges, many also let you prepay room and board costs. If you find a state plan that you like better than the one offered by your home state, you may be able to choose a different plan.

Now that you know the basics, it's time to answer the question: Does a prepaid tuition plan make sense for your family? This type of plan may be right for you if:

- You don't like risk and uncertainty

- You'll sleep better at night knowing that college tuition is guaranteed

- You don't expect to be eligible for financial aid

- The school, your child, wants to attend is covered by a prepaid plan

Remember, you've always got the option of investing in both a prepaid tuition plan and an ESA. Any costs not covered by the prepaid plan can be picked up by funds you've accumulated in the ESA, without affecting either tax advantages.

Education Bonds and CDs

For the past ten years or so, anxious parents have had the option to invest in safe, guaranteed college investment vehicles—specifically education bonds and college CDs—and they've largely passed them by. After all, when the stock market was going higher every day, it was easy to ignore options that simply plodded along without bringing back super-high returns. Now that the markets have seen big dips and the credit crunch has hit home, safe (but boring) investments suddenly have a lot more appeal.

They should, and not just because other investments have lost their allure. These college savings vehicles deserve a place in your college savings portfolio in every market. They serve as a safety net for your college savings, and they do provide returns—not exciting returns, but guaranteed steady returns. What you see is what you get.

Education Bonds

The U.S. Treasury wants your children to go to college, and to help you along; they created an Education Savings Bond Program, which is very similar to their plain old savings bond program. It's not just the name that sets these bonds apart, though; it's their tax treatment.

When you specifically buy an education savings bond (Series EE or Series I, as long as they were issued after 1989), your interest earnings will be at least partially (but usually completely) exempt from federal income tax. To be eligible for that favored tax treatment, which effectively ramps up your earnings, you have to jump through a few hoops:

- You have to pay for qualified education expenses with all of the bond proceeds (principal and interest) in the same year that you redeem the bonds.

- You have to be at least twenty-four years old when you buy the bond.

- You have to register the securities in your name if you plan to use them for yourself.

- You have to register them in your name or your spouse's name if you plan to use them for your children.

- If you're married, you have to file a joint tax return to get the tax break.

- You cannot list your child as a co-owner of the bond, only as a beneficiary.

On top of all that, the tax benefit is subject to income caps—if you make too much money, no tax-free interest. Your income is evaluated in the year you redeem the bonds, not the year you purchase them. For 2014, the tax break disappears for single taxpayers earning at least $84,950 and joint taxpayers earning at least $134,900. Only single taxpayers earning less than $69,950 and joint taxpayers earning less than $104,900 are qualify for the full benefit. These income thresholds are adjusted every year, so the levels by the time you pay for college expenses will likely look substantially different.

College Certificates of Deposit

You already know about regular bank certificates of deposit (CDs), but what you might not know is that there are special CDs whose sole purpose is education investing. Almost thirty years ago, the College Savings Bank created and introduced these targeted accounts called CollegeSure CDs. In some ways, they work just like regular CDs: For example, you deposit a lump sum of money for a specific long term, and you can't take that money out early without paying the penalty. However, CollegeSure CDs have something you won't find in plain old bank CDs—a college-oriented interest rate.

College Sure Guarantees

Unlike other types of college investments, College Sure CDs are guaranteed in two ways. First, these CDs are covered by FDIC insurance, so your money won't disappear. Second, your rate of return is guaranteed, so you don't have to worry that your returns will decline or disappear.

Interest in College Sure CDs is based on the Independent College 500 Index (created by the College Board). The index, as its name implies, tracks the average cost of 500 private schools. And the College Sure interest rate equals the average cost increase in those colleges. In fact, the rate is guaranteed to be no lower than that average, but it can be higher.

Here's how college CDs work as a college-savings vehicle. The big lump sum you deposit is the amount you would need to pay to send your kid to college now. Each "unit" (these CDs are measured in units) equals one year of all-inclusive college costs. Of course, you don't have to deposit the full amount all in one shot—you can buy pieces of units. The minimum deposit to open a unit is $500, and you can add to it in increments of $250 or more ($100 increments if you use an automatic monthly savings plan). Then, thanks to the index-based interest rate, that deposit will grow at the same rate as college costs.

RETIREMENT PLANNING

Your Golden Years

Do you think you're too young to start thinking about your retirement? Think again. People are living longer, which means you'll likely have quite a few golden years to enjoy. Get the most out of them by planning your future goals now. Numerous investment options will help you attain your goals. You can invest in employer-based plans, like a 401(k), or you can set up your own plan, like an IRA. Don't plan to rely on Social Security as your sole source of income for retirement.

Tax-Deferred Investing

Taxable investments require that you pay taxes on annual interest or dividends and on any profit on investments you sell. For instance, if you have a savings account, you'll be taxed on the interest it earns. Tax-deferred investments, on the other hand, offer you a way to avoid paying taxes on your current earnings, at least until you reach a certain age or meet other qualifications.

Tax-Exempt Investments

A tax-exempt (or tax-free) investment is one where current income earned on the investment is not taxed— for instance, most municipal bonds. Keep in mind that even tax-exempt investments aren't necessarily free of all taxes. Depending on the investment, you may be exempt only from certain taxes, like federal income tax or state and local taxes.

When you hold investments outside special tax-deferred accounts, you will likely be required to pay taxes on their earnings, both regular income (like interest and dividends) and capital gains. Virtually every type of investment is taxable on some level, from stocks to bonds to funds. Even real estate investments, businesses you own a piece of, and collectibles— basically, any investment you make where you can enjoy the profits (or suffer the losses) immediately (and not have to wait until sometime in the future)— can impact your current taxes.

If you have a tax-deferred investment and don't withdraw any money from the account, you don't pay taxes on it. Most of the time, the money you place into tax-deferred accounts will be at least partially, if not completely, tax-deductible right now. Of course, some exceptions apply, like Roth IRA contributions or contributions whose deductibility gets phased out based on your income level. Keep in mind that these accounts are meant to be used for large and specific financial goals, like education or retirement. If you withdraw money from these accounts too soon or use the money for other purposes, you can expect to pay some stiff penalties.

A big plus of tax-deferred investing is the ability to put pre-tax dollars into retirement accounts. For instance, with a 401(k) plan, your contribution to a tax-deferred retirement plan is deducted from your taxable income. This lets you invest money for the future that you would have otherwise paid to Uncle Sam. Let's say your income puts you in the 27 percent marginal income tax bracket, and your annual contribution to your tax-deferred retirement plan is $1,000. Your federal income taxes will drop by $270, or 27 percent of your retirement contribution. Your marginal tax rate (that is the rate you pay on your highest dollar of earnings) determines your savings.

Invest Early and Often

The earlier you begin investing, the more money you'll have for retirement. That's because you're giving your money more time to grow. On top of that, you have more time to ride out market downturns. With more time on your side, your retirement savings will have more time to rebound if the markets dive.

Consider the story of two twenty-five-year-olds, Madison and Cooper.

1. Madison invests $2,000 annually over ten years, stashing the money away in her company's 401(k) plan. Then she stops at age thirty-five, never adding another penny into her plan. Madison can expect an average 10 percent annual growth rate on her investments. Because she started early and gave her money time to grow before taking it out at retirement, she can cash out at age sixty-five with $556,197.

2. Starting at age thirty-four, Cooper socks $2,000 away in his 401(k) plan every year for the next thirty years. Cooper ends up putting away three times as much money as Madison. But his retirement stash—which has earned the same rate of return over the years—is just $328,988. That's much less— more than $225,000 less—than Madison's.

Both Madison and Cooper had the power of compound interest on their side. Madison harnessed it earlier and thus reaped higher gains. Here's the moral of the story: If you can afford to live without those tens or even hundreds of thousands of dollars in retirement, then, by all means, procrastinate.

The 401(k) Plan

For nearly twenty years, one of the most significant retirement investing tools has been the 401(k) plan. The 401(k) is set up by your employer and is designed to help you save (and build) money for retirement. The money you contribute to your 401(k) is pooled and invested in stocks, bonds, mutual funds, or other types of investments. You choose the type of investment from your company's list of options. Usually, your contribution is deducted from your paycheck before taxes and goes directly into your 401(k) account.

If such a plan is offered where you work, there is no reason not to jump at the opportunity. Putting the money in a plan earmarks it for your retirement, and you don't have to pay taxes on it as the money grows. In addition, employers generally make a matching contribution, which can be as much as 10, 25, or even 50 percent of the amount you contribute.

Contributions to 401(k)

A 401(k) plan can be set up by an employer in a number of different manners, with some going into effect immediately and others kicking in after you've worked in the company for a certain length of time. As of 2015, you can contribute up to $18,000 of your salary to your 401(k) plan in a given year.

There is a big difference between investing in a 401(k) and in a mutual fund that you can buy or sell at will. The IRS will not tax your 401(k) earnings as long as they remain invested in your 401(k). As soon as the money starts coming out, you'll start paying taxes on it. And if you withdraw money before a set date (usually when you reach fifty-nine and a half years of age), you may have to pay the penalty. With a current mutual fund investment, you'll pay taxes annually on the dividends, and capital gains your fund earns, whether you take the money out or let it continue to work for you.

Suppose your employer is making a matching contribution to your 401(k) of, say, 10 percent of what you put in. In that case, you already see a 10 percent growth on your investment, plus whatever gains the

total investment accrues over time. It is a simple solution to retirement planning that you do not have to set up yourself. However, you do need to keep tabs on where your 401(k) money is being invested. Too many people just make a choice and let it ride.

If you work in a nonprofit organization, you may be able to choose a 403(b) plan, which works similarly to a 401(k). Such plans generally have fewer investment options, but they are also tax-deferred. Government workers may be offered a 457 plan, which is also similar in principle to a 401(k) or 403(b), with some additional restrictions.

Your 401(k) Investing Strategy

Since you are in a retirement plan for the long haul, you need not worry too much about the days, weeks, or even months when the stock market is down. In fact, drops in the market can be in your favor as you continue to put money into the plan through payroll deductions. This concept, called dollar-cost averaging, enables you to buy more shares of a stock or mutual fund when the rate is lower. In the long term, of course, the market will go up, and all those inexpensive shares will increase in value.

Since a 401(k) plan is a long-term retirement vehicle, it's important that you remember your long-term goals and stick to them. Focus on the long term, and as you approach retirement,

maintain a solid assessment of how much money you will have when you retire and what your income will be. Besides Social Security benefits, you may have a pension plan and other savings.

All in all, the 401(k) plan is an excellent opportunity to build for your retirement and do so at the level you feel most comfortable. As one financial analyst puts it, "No matter what I say or suggest, the bottom line is that the individual has to be able to sleep comfortably at night." It all goes back to risk tolerance. First, be proactive and don't just forget about the money in your retirement plan; second, determine what level of risk is okay for your 401(k).

Keeping Your 401(k) Through Job Changes

Regardless of when, why, or how often you change jobs, your 401(k) investment can retain its tax-deferred status. If your new employer offers a 401(k), you can have your existing investment directly transferred or rolled over to a new account.

In a rollover, the money in your 401(k) is never in your possession, and you can thus avoid paying taxes on it (at least for the time being). It goes from your old employer to your new one; in industry lingo, from direct trustee to direct trustee.

By law, employers have to allow you to roll over your 401(k). If you take possession of the money yourself, the company will issue you a check for your investment less 20 percent, the

amount they're required to withhold and send to the IRS (where they treat it like an estimated tax payment) in case you don't roll the money over into another 401(k). You have to roll the money over within sixty days, or you'll be hit with taxes and penalties, and you have to deposit the full amount of your rollover—including replacing the 20 percent your company withheld to avoid having that amount considered an early (and taxable) distribution. If you are not starting a new job or are joining a company that does not have a 401(k) plan, roll over the money into an IRA.

Taking Money Out of a 401(k)

As soon as you hit age fifty-nine and a half, you're eligible to start making money (called distributions) out of your 401(k), whether you're formally retired or not. Once you hit age seventy and a half, you have to take out at least the minimum required distribution.

Sometimes people need to tap into their retirement funds early due to financial hardship, such as buying a primary residence, preventing foreclosure on your home, paying college tuition due in the next twelve months, or paying unreimbursed medical expenses. These withdrawals will cost you the full tax bill on the distribution plus a 10 percent penalty. You can escape the penalty under really extreme circumstances, but you'll always be stuck with the taxes. A better choice when you really need the money? A loan from your plan; many 401(k) plans allow loans, and there are no taxes or penalties at stake. The only caveat: the loan has to be repaid in full before you stop working for the employer who maintains the plan.

Individual Retirement Accounts (IRAs)

The most popular retirement plan of the last decade has certainly been the individual retirement account or IRA. Now available in two varieties—traditional and Roth—IRAs offer you a safe, tax-favored way for your money to grow for your retirement years. And now they're even safer: In April 2005, the U.S. Supreme Court unanimously ruled that IRAs are fully protected should you need to file for personal bankruptcy.

Traditional IRAs

You are allowed to contribute up to $5,500 per year to a traditional IRA (as of 2015). If you are married, you and your spouse may each contribute up to $4,000 into your own separate IRA accounts. If you are receiving alimony, you also qualify to contribute to an IRA. All or a segment of the contributions you make may be tax-deductible, but that depends on other factors like your adjusted gross income and other retirement contributions (if you participate in a qualified retirement plan through your job, for example). You'll have to closely examine the tax tables to determine the tax advantages a traditional IRA offers.

Once you are past fifty-nine and a half years of age, you can withdraw the money; when you reach seventy and a half, the government starts putting minimums on how much you need to withdraw annually. You pay income taxes on the investment earnings when making withdrawals, but the long period of tax-deferred income still outweighs this taxation. Also, it is very often the case that the income level for someone in her sixties, perhaps semiretired, is lower than it was in her forties, so she will fall into a lower tax bracket. Some experts feel that it makes sound financial sense to defer tax payment for another twenty years.

You can choose to start an IRA through a bank, brokerage house, or mutual fund. Traditionally, banks offer fewer options than brokerage houses, usually sticking with safer options such as CDs. Brokerage houses offer a wider range of options should you choose to be savvier with your IRA investment, or you can play it safe with a money market fund. Mutual funds are, by definition, supposed to be riskier than a CD or money market account. The long time frame of an IRA makes equities or equity funds more attractive for some investors. Like other investments, you can move your investments around within the IRA to suit your comfort level regarding risk.

Too many people put money into an IRA and don't do anything with it. There is often a feeling that because you cannot take it out until age fifty-nine and a half, you can't touch the money once it is in an IRA. That is not the case. There's nothing wrong with being proactive with the money you are investing within the IRA. In fact, you should be.

Roth IRAs

With this relatively new IRA, you are still limited to the same $5,500 annual investment ceiling. Your contributions to a Roth IRA are not tax-deductible; you pay taxes on every dollar that goes into one of these retirement accounts. When it comes time to take money out of this account, however, you will not be subject to any more taxes—ever!

In fact, there are very few regulations when it comes to withdrawing money from a Roth IRA. The money must be in the plan until you are at least fifty-nine and a half. However, you can withdraw up to $10,000 after five years, penalty-free, if you are using the money for qualifying first-time home-buying expenses, if you become disabled, or if the distribution is to a beneficiary upon the death of the original account owner.

Who Was Roth?

Roth IRAs are named for their creator, the late senator William Roth. Roth, a Republican from Delaware, sponsored legislation that would allow investors to pay taxes on their retirement savings upfront and withdraw them without paying additional taxes. It was part of the Taxpayer Relief Act of 1997, which went into effect on January 1, 1998.

Whereas the government eventually requires you to make minimum withdrawals from a traditional IRA, you can leave your money in a Roth IRA with no minimum distribution requirements. This can even allow for a large tax-free benefit to pass directly to your heirs if you so choose.

Your income determines your eligibility to contribute to a Roth IRA. This income structuring is subject to change at any time, so ask about your eligibility. As of 2015, the Roth option is phased out as adjusted gross income reaches between $116,000 and $131,000 for single filers and between $183,000 and $193,000 for joint filers.

It is possible to roll the money over from a traditional to a Roth IRA. The determination of whether to invest or rollover your money is based on your own financial situation. For current contributions, if you can't deduct a traditional IRA but still want to put some money away, go for the Roth (if you're eligible). Also, if you think your retirement tax rate will be higher or that you may need some of the money before retirement, a Roth IRA could be a better choice. As for the future, many experts agree that taking the tax hit now, if you can afford it, is far better than taking it on a much larger sum later on. Right now, the tax hit is a known quantity: the amount of your rollover times your marginal tax rate. The future tax hit is a question mark, as both the tax rates and income are unknown factors; almost certainly, though, that future tax hit will be bigger.

Health Savings Account

A health savings account (HSA) allows you to put money aside for medical expenses tax-free. You must have a special form of qualified health coverage called a high-deductible health plan— basically emergency health insurance that comes with a very high minimum deductible. The higher the deductible of your HDHP, the more you're allowed to save. The money you put into your HSA and all of the compounded earnings are yours until you die.

If you choose to roll over an existing IRA, simply call the company that holds your account and tell them. They'll talk with you about your unique tax situation and send you all the required paperwork to make the switch. Your accountant will be able to provide you with the most accurate tax information, including the possible need to adjust your withholding taxes or make some estimated tax payments.

Which Is Better?

Assuming you are eligible for both traditional and Roth IRAs, the biggest determining factor is whether it is to your benefit to take a deduction now and pay taxes later when you withdraw the money or to pay taxes on your contribution now and never worry about them again.

You must look at your own personal financial situation to determine which IRA is right for you. Nonetheless, websites have calculators and fancy ten-page sections devoted to figuring out the answer to this question. It shouldn't be all that complicated. And a good accountant should be able to help you figure it all out in less time than it takes to download and evaluate the calculation methods.

Investment Black Holes

In the late 1980s, the term "investment black holes" referred to the virtually complete disappearance of investment capital due to sudden heavy market losses. Since then, the market has seen the rise and fall of several of these market-shaking phenomena that rapidly cause enormous losses for investors. The 2008 markets saw similar shakeups and threw millions of investors into a massive panic.

The bottom line is that no matter how much you calculate, you cannot know for sure what the next thirty years have in store in terms of taxes, the rate of inflation, the cost of living, your own health, and the stability of your job. While it is to your advantage to put money away for your retirement years, the decision to choose the traditional or the Roth IRA is not as tough as it is made out to be. Either way, you will have saved money for your retirement years. If you qualify for both plans, the simple equation is whether it's to your benefit to take tax deductions now or whether you can afford not to and have benefits later on. Figure out basic, approximate numbers with your accountant, consider other factors in your life, make an

overall assessment of your future as you'd like it to be, and pick one. Since your future is not a certainty, go with your best assumption.

Stay Focused

No rule says you can't invest in both a 401(k) plan and an IRA. The most important point is to take advantage of all the tax-deferred investment opportunities you can. Start as early as you can and keep filling them up with the money, come rain or shine.

The future of Social Security looks uncertain at best—the shrinking number of younger workers means fewer workers are supporting each Social Security retiree. Compare the numbers: In 1950, sixteen workers were supporting each retiree, as opposed to three workers per retiree in 2000. The number continues to decrease. If you instead focus on tax-deferred investing, you'll be taking a crucial step toward building a safe, secure, and sustainable financial future.

Conclusion

The market is only a market, with no feeling and no connection attach to it. There's nothing exciting about this, nor is it particularly thrilling. For others, the major problem is that they choose to mess up the investment market with capital, or, more accurately, assets that they expect to buy.

Please step away from the pedestal, and turn aside from your feelings.

The more dispassionate and comparatively calm you are willing to keep with respect to capital market activities and machinations or any asset sector, the easier that will be with your overall investment effort.

To me, the best approach of this book will still be to go back to the fundamentals for the experienced traveler or for the novice. Have a clear idea of what type of business you're working with. For starters, if you plan to restrict your search to just the S&P 500 index stocks, then research such stocks and come to understand the behavior of the index like you might change your own body.

This, of course, may not happen immediately, and to strive for it will take regular, diligent action.

The next move will be to devise the hunting plan or hunting method with the clearness of the goals. This is where hundreds of people will be gunning for the simple way out, seduced by this or that ready-made machine offered by glib salespeople who pledge for a commitment of only one hour a day to roll in riches.

Little is really good for free. Only think of the duck swimming serenely on the lake's shore, when in reality, it is actively paddling to stay afloat under the waters. This, too, can be a harbinger about how the particular structure builds.

You can run into dead ends, and in anger, you can start pulling the hair out of its roots. That is completely natural. What counts most here will be the tenacious endeavor to build your own workable method. I can just advise you- don't give up. Eventually, you would be able to locate the framework because when you believe it and start seeing the steady benefits from it, even the struggles they followed, it would make their effort worth it.

It's my sincere wish that you might produce steady gains from the investment market, and who knows, maybe one day you'd be able to leave your day job and live to live entirely off the stock market income.

Never give up.